The Elephant In The Room

Practical solutions to 26 HR dilemmas

Donna Obstfeld
BSc FCIPD

3P
PUBLISHING

First published in 2022 in the UK

3P Publishing, C E C, London Road, Corby, NN17 5EU

A catalogue number for this book is available from the British Library

ISBN: 978-1-913740-53-5

Cover: James Mossop

The advice within these pages is a general guideline and should not be relied on as legal advice. Legislation and case law changes over time and varies between jurisdictions. Every business, situation and employee is different and it is important that you take specific advice from a trusted source who has all the information relevant to your specific scenario before giving advice.

To my two grandmothers:
Joyce (1923–2015) and
Dora (1918–2021)

Who were so very different from each other
but from whom I learnt so much about how to be me.

Thank you both for making my parents who they are.

And to my wonderful husband Joel
and our two amazing children, Jonathan and Dania.

Without the three of you, my life would not be complete
and there would be little point in doing what I do.

Thank you for ALWAYS being there for me.

CONTENTS

FOREWORD

People, eh? We can't succeed in business without them but boy can they cause us pain and grief. Every single business owner that has ever lived has had a problem with staff at some point.

I mean, just take a look at the chapter headings in this wonderfully crafted book. It's a minefield out there. And for many years it's felt like the legislators have had it in for all us entrepreneurs as more laws, rules and regulations have been heaped upon us and employees have gained more and more rights and protections. So the 'HR' industry has never been more buoyant.

Now my own experience of 'HR consultants' has been that they consistently - and persistently - fail to live in the real world. So often their advice is theoretical and completely impractical. But this book's not like that.

It's possible that the book you are now reading is the single most practical book ever written on the management of people in the workplace. Seriously.

It's a handy little guide to keep in the top drawer of your desk, ready for the day when you need it. Because you will need it.

The advanced copy that Donna kindly sent me has become like a fire extinguisher to me. You know what I mean. Most of the time I don't need it, but when I do it just might save my business. It's like those health and safety signs that you see on construction sites: '78 days without an accident".

Well, you can start your own tally now. How many days till you need this book? I hope it's hundreds and hundreds. But experience tells me that you'll need it sooner than you think. Bloody staff!

Well at least with this book you know how to have the conversations, and where you stand – which makes it well worth the cover price (and a lot cheaper than a fire extinguisher!).

So thank you Donna for being so practical. For tackling the elephants. And equipping us so brilliantly.

On behalf of business owners everywhere, but especially those of us with staff, we salute you.

Nigel Botterill
Entrepreneur and employer of 52 souls

INTRODUCTION

There is no getting away from it. While I don't get the same reaction as estate agents or recruitment consultants, when I tell people I am in HR, I am usually greeted by a groan, told HR is a waste of space and asked, 'Why?'

That's a really good question and one I have answered in different ways over the last 25 years. I know I don't fit the stereotype of an HR person, and I don't think I ever have! At a local networking meeting, I was talking to an insolvency practitioner, who I had just met for the first time. We were discussing a couple of projects I had done which although were HR-led, were essentially business turnaround projects. Someone else came to join our circle and the insolvency practitioner introduced me to the newcomer saying, 'she does HR, but she is not your typical HR lady.' I took that as a compliment. In just a few minutes he got me and he got the reason I do HR. The business comes first… without the business, there is no HR.

So, what exactly is HR? If you ask my husband, HR stands for Human Remains. He doesn't have a good opinion of the profession – and he is not alone!

HR has been given many names over the years and the evolution of the profession has taken place as the nature of employees in business has changed. The profession has kept up with the times, and as employment law has evolved, the work of the HR professional has changed from time and motion studies, through an era of tea and tissues to one of administrator, manager and business partner. In traditional businesses and organisations, HR rarely sits at the top table, but in the more forward-thinking organisations HR is viewed as a strategic partner and is increasingly expected to contribute to the overall success of the organisation.

3

The name of the profession has also changed over time from Workforce Management to Personnel and almost to Human Capital Management, but that phrase melted away, leaving us with the commonly used but often misunderstood Human Resources. Today, terms such as people and culture, people operations, talent management and employee experience are all in use by companies across the globe as they try to differentiate themselves from their competitors and position themselves as employers of choice.

To me, whatever it is called, the role of HR is to support both the employer and the employees within a business or organisation. To do so effectively, HR professionals must walk a metaphorical tightrope as they balance the often conflicting needs of the business, managers, employees and other stakeholders.

I am writing this book on the assumption that the people reading it are business owners and managers who need to manage their staff in the absence of a professional HR department; and while there are lots of places out there that you can get information, advice, help and support, it may be a case of 'you don't know what you don't know'. That said, I don't want to exclude interested managers and owners of larger businesses! At the end of the day, employment law and its application does not change based on the size of the business or the number of employees; it is arguably just the impact and costs that differ.

This book will also be relevant to you whatever the nature of your business. Whether you are a charity, a school, a medical practice, a retailer, a Fintech start-up, a professional practice or a manufacturer, the law does not change, it is just the implementation of policies and procedures that may need to be approached differently to match the specific nuances of your sector.

This book is designed to point you in the right direction and to ensure the advice you are getting, whether from internal or external resources, is robust and business appropriate. By the time you have read it, you will hopefully know where you need help, and what you can do safely yourself.

My philosophy is you understand the situation you are in, the risks to your business of the different approaches and are able to take an informed decision for each situation. Despite what the employment lawyers and some of the HR helplines will have you believe, every situation has multiple solutions and as a business owner you need to understand the options, the pros and cons of the approaches available to you and then make a decision based on your business, your culture and values, your finances, your time, the employee/employees involved, your personality, the strengths of your team (if you have one) and your approach to risk. There is definitely not a one-solution-fits-all approach to managing people. I like to consider people management as a fine balance between art and science.

Start as you mean to go on

My earliest memories include the world of work. I learnt the ethos of work on the skirts of my mother, quite literally.

While I was growing up, my parents ran a food supplies business supplying hotels and caterers with unusual products. It was not uncommon for us to have a dinner made up of whatever came out of the unmarked tin. Where labels had come off, the products couldn't be sold and therefore they came home and we got to eat them. In addition to that there were exotic treats that were hidden away in the back of the cupboard for 'special' occasions – the plums in chocolate, a Polish delicacy was my favourite. I am delighted that, with the rise in Polish shops around the UK, I have now been able to find the delicacy of my childhood.

My parents ran their business from home and an offsite warehouse. They had a number of vans and lorries, and I have very clear recollections of doing deliveries to hotels or restaurants with my mother when a driver was off or there was an unexpected urgent order. Customer service was paramount.

Now, my memories, as you may have worked out, are from the early to mid-'70s. In those days, much to my children's horror, there were no mobile phones or cordless phones and the concept of a VoIP (Voice over Internet Protocol) phone was just sci-fi. We had a plugged-in BT phone and just a single line, for home and work purposes. We were lucky enough to have multiple extension points, so there was a phone in the hall, my parents' bedroom and the 'office' (spare room). However, from the age of three or four years old, I remember being 'trained' to answer the phone professionally: '2126. Who's speaking, please?' Interestingly, having recently listened to Geoff

Burch's, *Go it Alone*[1], my parents were spot on. The way in which the phone is answered when you run a business, even if you are in the bathroom or in the middle of cooking dinner, is essential. There was a branded pen and paper by every phone and I had to take a message. If there were hard names, I was taught to ask them to spell them out and I recited it back to ensure the message was accurate. The same was the case with the phone number. If you listen to me on the phone now, there is no doubt I was trained to answer the phone properly and this habit has stuck (although I can generally spell the names ok now).

Another early lesson was that of filing. Computers did not exist in most businesses and everything had to be produced on a typewriter, so if you wanted multiple copies, you generally used carbon paper or went to a photocopy shop. Invoices in my parents' business were handwritten on quadruplicate paper where each page was a different colour – white, green, pink and yellow. Each invoice also had a sequential number on it. My task was sometimes to separate the invoices, but more often than not to file them in the appropriate file 'in the right order'. I learnt number ordering before I really understood the concept of addition or subtraction. I just had to know that five was bigger than two and that the number in front was just as important as the number at the end. There were office copies, warehouse copies and client copies and they all had to be in the right order, in the right place at the right time so that my parents, the warehouse man and the customers all had the information they needed and were happy.

All of these early skills are still the basics of business today, although technology has enabled us to come a very long way.

Fast-forward 30 years…

---

[1] Geoff Burch, *Go it Alone: The Streetwise Secrets of Self Employment. 2003*

Meet the herd

On 1st May 2021, my HR Practice, DOHR, celebrated 14 years in business. This book has grown from a series of blogs I wrote to mark its birthday. You need to bear with me for this one...

The traditional 14th anniversary gift is ivory. Today, in our much more conscientious world of conservation and environmental awareness, ivory is no longer acceptable, so the concept has evolved into giving an ivory-coloured gift, elephant-related presents or making a donation to a charity for elephant protection.

A few years ago, I was privileged to meet several herds of wild elephants at Addo Elephant National Park in South Africa. They left a lasting impression on me. Living in complex social groups led by a matriarch, elephants are smart, sensitive and self-aware, displaying complex emotions, including compassion, humour and grief. Little wonder they traditionally symbolise stability, wisdom, patience and dignity – all characteristics that chime with HR best practice.

Looking for further ways in which I could link the elephant to the world of HR, I discovered 13 phrases that particularly resonated:

1. An elephant never forgets. (English proverb)
2. Do not compare a fly with an elephant. (Greek proverb)
3. To make an elephant out of a mosquito. (Dutch proverb)
4. If you're going to move, move like an elephant, not like a hyena. (African proverb)
5. There is only one way to eat an elephant – one bite at a time. (Archbishop Desmond Tutu)
6. Nature's great masterpiece, an elephant; the only harmless great thing. (John Donne)

7. Awake. Be the witness of your thoughts. The elephant hauls himself from the mud. In the same way, drag yourself out of your sloth. (Buddha)
8. As an elephant in the battlefield withstands arrows shot from bows all around, even so, shall I endure abuse. (Buddha)
9. When there is an invisible elephant in the room, one is, from time to time, bound to trip over a trunk. (Karen Joy Fowler)
10. Owning a business is like owning an elephant. (Hugh Williams)
11. They say an elephant never forgets. What they don't say is that you never forget an elephant. (Bill Murray)
12. An elephant does not find its own trunk heavy. (Zakes Mda)
13. The elephant in the room. (English idiom)

The one that leapt out for me was, of course, 'the elephant in the room'. For employers, the elephants in the room are all the things they don't want to talk about or deal with, sometimes because they are embarrassed, but often because they simply don't know how.

And then I found the 14th quote, from the late Prof. Randy Pausch: 'When there's an elephant in the room, introduce him.'

And so the blogs were born.

This book expands on the issues discussed in the original blogs, and includes case studies, specific signposting to best practice, useful tips and resources. You might not agree with some of the views expressed. That's ok; areas of disagreement simply reflect the reality of a diverse workplace and society. All I ask is that you aren't disagreeable in your disagreement. Be kind, be curious. Seek to understand and accept that the world is a richer place because of our differences.

Above all, if you are affected by or dealing with any of the issues discussed in the following pages, you are not alone. Professional help is available. Never be afraid to seek it out.

Donna Obstfeld
February 2022

MALODOROUS ELEPHANTS

'Once you wake up and smell the coffee, it's hard to get
back to sleep.'
Fran Drescher

Cigarettes

In 2019, 13.9% of adults in England smoked.[2]

In my opinion, there is nothing worse than a colleague who comes into a meeting stinking of cigarettes. I remember a time when people used to smoke in offices and it was completely normal. Just like smoking sections on an aeroplane – smokers on the left or at the back, non-smokers at the front or on the right – my kids can't believe this was ever a thing.

I also remember the introduction of 'the smoking room', the small office that had become a fume-ridden hole into which those who partook were invited to inhale stale air and other people's tobacco smog. Even the smokers hated the smoking room.

Today, those who want to smoke must do so outside, often in designated areas. The problem is, and has always been, what happens when they return to the office, with the stench of cigarettes on their clothes and their breath.

In reality, there is nothing an employer can do about it. It is not illegal to smoke. In the UK, smoking is a right, but where you can smoke is regulated. Whether smoking is a problem in the workplace depends only on who is around the smoker when they return after a smoking break.

Some people, like me, may be allergic to cigarette smoke. I can tell a mile off if someone has been smoking. It usually starts with me coughing uncontrollably until I figure out why. (The same thing happens with some perfumes and hand creams, as my staff will tell you.) Other people may just dislike the smell or find it unprofessional in a business environment.

---

[2] ethnicity-facts-figures.service.gov.uk/health/alcohol-smoking-and-drug-use/adult-smokers/latest

Addressing the elephant

As the business owner, employer or line manager, it's your role to balance the needs of the smoker, their colleagues and the business.

You have a duty of care towards all your staff, and part of that is to create an environment where everyone feels physically and psychologically safe. Conflict in the workplace should be nipped in the bud at the earliest opportunity. Communication and discussion need to form the basis of dealing with concerns, and outcomes need to be agreed, communicated and enforced.

So, what to do with your smoker vs non-smoker?

One frequent bone of contention for non-smokers is the extra time their smoking colleagues spend on cigarette breaks. In 2017, a Japanese marketing firm granted non-smokers an extra six days' annual leave to make up for the time they didn't spend on cigarette breaks. As the company was based on the 29th floor, a 'quick' break took at least 15 minutes. Some businesses get around this problem by granting everyone a one-hour 'lunch' break, which smokers may divide into several shorter blocks. This ensures each employee has the same amount of rest time every day.

Then there is the smell, whether it's from a traditional tobacco-based cigarette or a scented e-cigarette. To mitigate this, one client of mine puts gum and body spray in the toilets and actively encourages people to freshen up after a smoking break. Good ventilation will also help, besides reducing the risk of infections, including Covid-19 and flu. If people put on a coat or a jumper to smoke outside, removing the item and leaving it in an area away from the desks or the main workspace may be another way to minimise the transfer of cigarette smells coming back into the office where it may make some staff feel uncomfortable.

Whatever approach you decide to take, fairness, consistency and communication are going to be essential. If there is a problem, find a way to talk about it. Ask staff for their input constructively and openly. Ensure that the smokers understand the impact they are having on the non-smokers and that the non-smokers appreciate that smokers have a right to smoke.

Additional information

Smoking in the workplace has been prohibited in all but a handful of situations since 2007 to protect against the dangers of second-hand smoke. However, there is currently no equivalent legal restriction on the use of electronic or e-cigarettes. It's up to individual employers to decide on their own policy, although all of our clients are consistent between tobacco and e-cigarettes.

If employees are given vaping breaks, they must not be expected to take these in a designated smoking area, as this would put them at risk of passive smoking.

GOV.UK: gov.uk/smoking-at-work-the-law

Smokefree England: smokefreeengland.co.uk/what-do-i-do/business

Action on Smoking and Health: ash.org.uk/information-and-resources/briefings/will-you-permit-or-prohibit-e-cigarette-use-on-your-premises

Alcohol

Today, 8th July 2021, the WHO reported 6,305 alcohol-related deaths.[3]

In some sectors, drinking (alcohol) at work is part of the job – in fact, it's expected. Journalism, marketing, sales and City trading are all occupations that have traditionally encouraged, or even required, people to build their networks and work their magic in the pub or the wine bar.

Most companies, however, have a policy that states you must not attend work under the influence of alcohol and some will not permit drinking during working hours, which may include business lunches, networking events and formal dinners.

Policy notwithstanding, how do you manage and support an employee who sometimes or frequently comes into work smelling of alcohol?

Addressing the elephant

There are several points you need to consider before taking action:

- Whether you have documented rules, policies or procedures around alcohol and attending work under the influence
- Whether the employee is in a safety-critical role or holds a licence that requires them to be sober
- Examples of this may be a forklift truck licence or a security guard's SIA licence
- Whether the drinking is a result of work-related stress
- Whether the drinking is a result of poor mental health

---

[3] www.worldometers.info

You have no idea what you are dealing with at this stage, other than a bad smell, so don't jump to conclusions. The person may be aware of the smell but be too embarrassed to seek help – or they may indeed have a genuine alcohol problem, the symptoms and cause of which need to be addressed. They might have diabetic ketoacidosis (DKA), which requires medical attention, or they might be in dietary ketosis on a carbohydrate-restricted diet. In either situation, their breath may smell like acetone, which is very similar to stale alcohol.

The most important thing is to keep an open mind and not be judgemental. You are on a fact-find to establish what the problem is, so don't make assumptions.

Find a suitable time and place to have an open, supportive conversation. Address your concerns directly, so that the elephant is visible to you and your colleague. Demonstrate your concerns with a few examples, but don't make it overwhelming. If work quality has been impacted, say so. If it hasn't, make sure that they know this, too.

Your role is to provide a safe place to talk and, if they do have an alcohol problem, to help them get professional help. You can't solve all their problems. You're not trained to do so, and it's not your job to do so. However, you do have a duty of care towards them and others, and ignoring the problem won't make it go away. If they are client-facing, training younger or less experienced members of staff, or line-managing others, they are representing your business. That is your reputation on the line, as well as theirs.

If you establish that an employee does have a problem with alcohol, you need to be mindful of any business events that might involve drinking. Beer Bust Fridays, Christmas drinks or team-building cocktail nights might be particularly difficult times for these employees. Ensuring that you have suitable drinks available for everyone at every event is really important. Not everyone drinks, perhaps as a result of personal choice, diet, medical or religious reasons, and you need to ensure that no one feels excluded, singled out or self-conscious because they are not drinking alcohol.

Additional information

While there is no specific law against drinking alcohol in many work environments, such as offices or retail, it is illegal for employees who drive or operate machinery as part of their job.

Alcohol dependency is not regarded as a disability under the Equality Act 2010. However, if it arises from specific mental or physical health issues, or has led to a serious condition such as liver disease, bear in mind that those issues and conditions might be classed as disabilities in their own right.

Alcohol Concern: alcoholchange.org.uk

Drinkaware: drinkaware.co.uk

Cannabis

Some 7.8% of people aged 16–59 reported using cannabis in 2019, including 18.7% of 16-24-year-olds.[4]

Some people can clock the smell of cannabis a mile off. Others might not realise what it is but will certainly be aware that it's an unusual aroma in the workplace.

Cannabis – also known as weed, marijuana, skunk, pot, spliff, grass, blow, puff and dope – is a class B drug in the UK under the Misuse of Drugs Act 1971. Possession can lead to an unlimited fine, up to five years in prison or both, while supplying can result in a 14-year sentence. In reality, anyone caught by the police with small quantities for personal use is unlikely to be arrested for a first offence.

As an employer, you are likely to have a zero-tolerance policy on drugs in the workplace. There are lots of sound reasons for this – some legal, some moral and some operational.

An employee who smells of cannabis may be using it for pleasure or relief from stress or pain. Alternatively, they could be dealing. Whatever the reason, this is an issue you can't ignore. You must have a conversation about your concerns. The smell is the symptom and a signal that you need to act fast. Don't wait for the impact – that's like trying to shut the cage door after the elephant has charged through it.

It will often be other members of staff who bring cannabis use to your attention as either a concern or a complaint – especially if the user's behaviour, judgement or productivity is disrupting their colleagues' work.

---

[4] ONS, March 2020

Addressing the elephant

Sometimes the best approach is to have an open conversation. Ask the employee why you can smell cannabis on them. Explain that the issue has been raised with you by other people in the business, without giving their names. I advocate a questioning approach, where you take the employee down a funnel with questions designed to get the employee to identify the problem, the impact and the outcome.

An example of this technique might be:

- 'Can you tell me why you think we are talking today?'
- 'Would it be a surprise if I told you I've had complaints from your colleagues about the smell of weed?'
- 'Could you tell me why you think this might be an issue?'
- 'What do you think the impact of this on your colleagues might be?'
- 'What do you think the impact on your work or your reputation might be?'
- 'If you were in my situation, what would you do?'

In other cases, it may be best to move straight to a disciplinary via a proper investigation. If you take this route, stick to the company policy and ensure you have strong evidence gathered in accordance with it. If you are using images or video, you must have a policy that tells people you are recording them at work. Only carry out a locker search or check personal possessions if there is a policy in place allowing you to do so. In this situation, any complaints or witness statements should be used, with witness permission.

The outcome of a disciplinary process can range from no action to termination, with a number of penalties in between.

The key is to follow your own policies and procedures at all times and to be consistent between employees.

Additional information

Medical cannabis was legalised in the UK in late 2018, although obtaining a prescription is extremely challenging. CBD oil is legal in the UK, as long as it is produced from EU-certified industrial hemp that contains less than 0.2% THC (tetrahydrocannabinol – the principal psychoactive component of cannabis). At such low levels, THC will not cause a high, and most drug tests cannot detect it.

Drug dependency is not regarded as a disability under the Equality Act 2010. However, if it arises from specific mental or physical health issues, or has caused a serious illness, bear in mind that those issues and illness might be classed as disabilities in their own right.

More information is available via the Frank (drug dependency information) website: talktofrank.com

Stories from the wild –
Drug and alcohol testing

Sitting on the floor

In September 2003 I was working for Metronet SSL. This was a Public Private Partnership (PPP) which had come out of London Underground. I did a five-month stint with them covering an HR Manager who had taken a sabbatical. I was six months pregnant and travelling around the network to the various depots. On an autumnal Friday afternoon in September, I was at Upminster on the District Line. My job on this occasion was to manage the drug and alcohol testing programme. In the morning, I pulled off a list of 25 employees on the afternoon shift at Upminster. Ten of these people needed to be randomly tested for drugs and alcohol. All of them were male and they were working maintaining the trains. I turn up unannounced and meet the tester from the external company. I present myself to the shift manager, who is not happy to see me, and I give him the names of the first two people on the list. One is off sick, the other is called in. I'm not allowed to give more than two names at a time and I am not allowed to tell the shift manager if his name is on the list. Although everyone knows the rules for drug and alcohol testing, as HR we are immediately the enemy. We have secrets (names) and we are not willing to share. The shift was due to end at 6, but staff could only go home once they had been tested, but I could only call two at a time. We are pulling workers off the job; we have the power to stand them down from duty;

we have the ability to send people straight to Occupational Health at head office in Marylebone. As a heavily trade unionised organisation, we are also having to contend with the union reps, some of whom also need testing.

On this particular afternoon, I ended up onsite for five hours, testing 10 people. Now bearing in mind that we need them to pee in a bottle and breathe into a container, five hours was a very long time. If people are off sick, or on annual leave, then they are of course exempt, which is why so many names are on the list and only 10 need testing, but for the rest there is no avoiding the test.

Policy is absolutely key here and so is communication. Everyone knows what the policy is and that to do their job, they must be 'clean' at all times. The policies had been in place for years, they are part of the employment contract and part of the union agreement. So why do people kick off when called in? Because they are human. Because it was not convenient.

One person had arranged to leave work half an hour early to catch a flight to go away for the weekend. The shift manager had to check with me whether they employee could leave. His name was on the list, but I couldn't tell them that and all I could say was that all staff currently on shift had to remain on site until I had all the required samples – it really wasn't very helpful, friendly or collaborative – but those were the rules that everyone had signed up to and I had to follow them. I could only call people in the order in which they appeared on the list until I had 10 samples. The shift manager understandably felt undermined and started yelling at me. He was going to call his union rep; I asked him to do so. He started waving policies and procedures at me; I asked him to read them. He stomped around and was in a filthy mood, but he really should have known better. Not only was the travelling employee called for testing, but also the shift manager himself was called for testing.

While most of the required samples were provided without too many problems, one employee really did struggle. Others came, produced their sample and went, but this particular employee just couldn't, or perhaps wouldn't, pee in the pot. I got to the point where this employee was the final sample, so I let everyone else go home, apart from the shift manager who needed to stay until I was finished. I read the rules again. I sat on the floor on 'guard duty' outside the toilet to ensure he didn't abscond. I provided cups of water. I read the rules again. I discussed the situation with the shift manager who by now had calmed down and accepted that I was just doing my job and that we did have a problem with one of his team. I called Occupational Health for guidance and the tester assured me that he had seen this before.

We had until 7pm before we could conclude that the employee was unable to produce a sample. By this time, my entire family were at my house to celebrate by husband's birthday with a traditional Friday Night Dinner! I'd already called my mum and asked her to pick my two-year-old up from nursery. I called her again and asked her to start making dinner - she'd already found my notes and lists for the menu, food prep etc. She'd set the table and started to cook the chicken. There I was, six months pregnant with 20 people due at my house for dinner and I was stuck sitting on the floor outside a toilet cubicle in Upminster depot, waiting for a guy to pee in a pot.

At 7pm, I called it. I asked him to meet me and his manager in the office. I sent the tester home and I started to fill in the paperwork. I was standing him down from duty until Monday morning. He had to report to Occupational Health at 7am for testing and he couldn't work Saturday or Sunday (another headache for the shift manager).

Eventually I got home at 8:30. The house was full, my mother put a plate of food in front of me and I got to celebrate my husband's birthday.

Body odour

Different people harbour different bacteria in their armpits and other bodily crevices, resulting in different smells, from sour, meaty and oniony to rotten egg.[5]

This is perhaps the ultimate in difficult workplace conversations and one we have had to support a lot of employers through over the years. Unlike most malodorous situations, where the employee usually has some control over the smell, body odour is something over which many people have little or no control.

In my experience, few cases of body odour result from someone not washing regularly. In most cases, the underlying issue is medical – due to, for example, hormonal changes, stress, hyperidrosis, bladder incontinence, acid reflux or gum disease – and the employee is both aware of and very embarrassed by their smell. Mental health issues may also be an underlying cause.

Broaching the subject of body odour with an employee requires tact, diplomacy and sensitivity. Be aware that the line manager or business owner may not be the best person to lead this conversation. Sometimes, an emotionally astute colleague may need to be asked to intervene.

The most tactless solution I've seen was a bottle of deodorant left in a brown paper bag on the employee's desk. The best was gym membership being offered to all staff to allow the employee access to showers and changing facilities during the day. However, even with this approach, how do you encourage the person with the problem to use the facilities?

---

[5] psychologytoday.com/gb/blog/the-red-light-district/201905/10-eye-opening-facts-about-body-odor

Addressing the elephant

It all boils down to a conversation.

I often start difficult conversations by asking questions. In this instance, something along the lines of:

- 'Do you have any idea why I wanted to chat with you today?'
- Or, 'Would it surprise you to know that your colleagues are concerned about you?'

An alternative approach may be to tell a story. This can work particularly well if the person broaching the subject has had their own experiences of body odour or knows someone who has.

It's important to recognise that you can't solve the problem. Your role is to make the employee aware of the concern and the fact that they need to address it. You need to establish what you as an employer can do to assist, which could range from providing or upgrading changing facilities to sitting the person by an opening window. Conversely, they may need to seek medical support, change their diet or alter their behaviours.

The remedy will be different in each particular case, but what you need to remember above all is that, as an employer, you cannot allow an employee to be bullied, harassed or excluded because of their smell. You have a duty of care to protect them and their colleagues. Your aim is to make your workplace a comfortable place to be for everyone.

Additional information

Body odour has its own page on the NHS website with a list of dos and don'ts. If you have ongoing concerns about an employee, they should be encouraged to visit their pharmacist or GP. In the most extreme circumstances, patients can be given injections into their armpits or even have their sweat glands removed.

NHS: nhs.uk/conditions/body-odour-bo

PROTECTED ELEPHANTS

*'What sets you apart can sometimes feel like a
burden and it's not.
A lot of the time, it's what makes you great.'*

Emma Stone

Protected elephants also known as protected characteristics

Although I have called this section 'protected elephants', I am in fact talking about 'protected characteristics'. This is a legal term (I am not a lawyer and I don't expect most business owners to be), but it is so important to the welfare of your team and the risks that you expose your business to that I am giving you a quick guide to the key terms.

What are the protected characteristics?

Protected characteristics are things which make you who you are and differentiate you from or group you with others who you work with. They are elements that mean you must not be treated any less favourably than other company employees because of one of these characteristics.

The nine protected characteristics are:

- Age
- Disability
- Gender
- Gender reassignment
- Sexual orientation
- Marriage and civil partnership
- Pregnancy and maternity
- Race
- Religion or belief

What is less favourable treatment?

Less favourable treatment is when one person feels or believes that they are in some way worse off than other people in their company as a result of being 'different'. It is worth understanding that intention and perception are very important and it is not how the 'perpetrator' intended to make the 'victim' feel, but how the 'victim' felt that matters. So if an employee is feeling bullied by their line manager, it is irrelevant whether the manager intended to bully the employee, bullying has occurred.

Getting the terminology right when talking about protected characteristics is really important, so I am briefly explaining them here before we look at each of the characteristics in turn.

Bullying

This may be a regular pattern of behaviour or a one-off occurrence of unwanted behaviour that makes someone feel uncomfortable, frightened, disrespected, humiliated, threatened or upset. Bullying can take many different forms, including spoken or written words, images, gestures, jokes and banter and physical behaviour.

Harassment

Bullying becomes harassment when it is linked to one of the protected characteristics. Not all bullying is harassment, but most harassment is also bullying. Harassment occurs when someone's dignity is violated or their working environment feels hostile. The person being affected does not need to be able to identify the behaviour as harassment for it to be illegal. Employers have a legal responsibility to act on all harassment whether they have seen it, the affected employee has reported or a third party has reported it.

Harassment may occur: when the person being harassed is thought to have a protected characteristic, whether or not they do; if they are linked to someone who is thought to have a protected characteristic, whether or not they do; or if they witness harassment and are upset by it.

Discrimination

Discrimination occurs when the employee is treated unfairly as a result of a protected characteristic. This might be in terms of recruitment, development, promotion, rota hours, opportunity, the nature of the work or work-related events such as socials.

Direct discrimination

In the case of direct discrimination, the employee is treated unfairly because they have the characteristic, or are thought to have the characteristic. Direct discrimination is also deemed to have occurred if the employee is associated with someone with the characteristic, such as a family member.

Indirect discrimination

Indirect discrimination occurs when policies, procedures or arrangements are applied to a group of people but affect some in an adverse way because of a protected characteristic.

Victimisation

In an employment law context, victimisation means that an employee is treated unfairly, bullied or discriminated against because they made or supported a complaint, or were thought to have done so, in connection with a protected characteristic.

Age

When Buster Martin died in 2011, aged 104, he was the oldest employee in the UK, still turning up for work every day to clean vans for a plumbing company in London.[6]

What is 'young'? What is 'old'? When does one stop being 'young' and become 'old'? Is there anything in between these states and, if so, how long can one dwell in such a space? Age tells us a lot about someone, but it also tells us nothing. It certainly pays not to make assumptions about people based on their age.

In the post-pandemic workplace, there is a lot of concern about age, including:

- Younger employees not having the education or the skills
- Older employees being too expensive
- Younger staff not having the right or enough experience
- Older staff having the wrong type of experience

While it's not unlawful for a potential or current employer to ask about age, it is unlawful for them to make decisions based on age. On this basis, many hiring employers don't even bring it up, because they want to avoid the risk of an age-discrimination complaint from someone before they even join the business.

Likewise, if an employer makes decisions about promotions, roles, redundancy or termination based on age, they will be breaking the law and potentially face age discrimination claims.

It gets even more complex when comments are made that imply an age-related decision, for example:

---

[6] sellpension.co.uk/the-worlds-oldest-workers

- 'We are looking for a junior who can be trained up.'
- 'We are looking for a senior to take the lead.'
- 'We think you will be better suited to a more traditional office culture.'
- 'Our newer hires can do that work in a fraction of the time.'

Addressing the elephant

It all comes down to creating a culture in which everyone feels valued, regardless of their age.

People must be offered jobs and allowed to thrive in those positions based on their performance and independent of their age. Although experience does come into it; a 20-year-old who has been working since they left school at 16 may be more capable than a 25-year-old with lots of academic qualifications, but little or no work or management experience.

In an attempt to remove the risk of age discrimination, it has been suggested that businesses recruit 'age blind' – removing education dates, employment dates and so on from the CV or application form. In my experience, this isn't the best way to solve the problem. It simply leads to interviewers trying to work out the person's age based on other clues (such as checking if they have GCSEs or O-levels), potentially jumping to the wrong conclusions and discriminating by accident as a result – what is called assumed age discrimination.

I, for one, am useless at identifying people's ages. I was once asked for present ideas for a man who was turning 100. It was a bit of a shock as I would have put money on him being no older than his mid-70s. I only ever saw him on his feet all day, teaching children to play chess – he could give feedback on every game, move-for-move, showing them where they had gone wrong or where they had switched the play in their favour.

It just goes to show that the saying, 'don't judge a book by its cover', can cut both ways where age is concerned.

Until April 2011, the default retirement age in the UK was 65 (coinciding with the state pension age for men), which meant employers could force workers to retire when they reached their 65th birthday. Since women could then access their state pensions at 60, they'd generally finish work five years before their male colleagues.

Today, there is no retirement age (and the state pension age has increased to 67 for anyone born after 5th March 1961). This makes things difficult when an employee can no longer do their job due to their physical or mental ageing; the only way to remove them is to performance-manage them out of the business, usually through the company's capability or disciplinary processes. Unless handled with great tact by the employer, this can be horrible for both sides, especially when the employee has been a fantastic worker for years. Even trying to hold a without-prejudice conversation can end up as a claim for bullying, harassment or age discrimination.

Every situation will be different. Understanding why the employee is still working may hold the key to figuring out how to retire them gracefully. Speaking to colleagues or even family members may provide you with insight to inform your discussions. Again, care needs to be taken not to upset or offend, as this could result in an age discrimination claim.

Additional information

Some larger organisations routinely run pre-retirement workshops and invite all employees over 55 to attend. The content is usually educational, including moving to part-time hours, understanding pensions, financial planning, will-writing, getting involved in the community and finding hobbies.

With this approach, the risk of an age discrimination claim is reduced (although not removed) because no employee is being singled out. The additional benefit is that it can help employees who may be worried that retirement is all about loss – of purpose, routine, dignity and independence – to reframe it in terms of the opportunities it offers.

Age UK has more useful information on retirement: ageuk.org.uk

Disability

Some 8.4 million people of working age (16–64) reported they were disabled in October–December 2020 – that's 20% of the working-age population.[7]

Starting with the assumption that a disabled person can do the job, has done it before and has a proven track record, would you employ them? If not, why not?

Might your answer depend on:

- Their type of disability – for example, if they are deaf, blind, a wheelchair user or an amputee?
- Your location and working environment?
- If they have the disability when they join you or develop it while they are with you?

The Equality Act 2010 makes it illegal to treat people less favourably than others as a result of their disability, and that extends to the workplace.

Employers have a legal obligation to make reasonable adjustments to enable people with disabilities to work effectively within a business and to have the same opportunities as their colleagues for training, career progression and reward. The challenge we always face is in defining what is reasonable. If there is a cost involved, is it affordable? Is there a lot of disruption? Are there any health and safety issues?

I have met, worked with and supported people with a huge range of disabilities over the past 25 years, and I'm pleased to say that, on the whole, attitudes have improved massively. Legislation has been updated, there is better training, technology has provided solutions that may not have existed

---

[7] House of Commons Briefing Paper, May 2021

even five years ago, and businesses are more willing to consider employing people with disabilities, but there is still a long way to go.

Recent government research shows that from October to December 2020, 8.4 million people of working age (16–64) reported being disabled – that's 20% of the working population, and an increase of 327,000 on the previous year. Around 4.4 million or 52.3% were in work, compared to 81.1% of people without a disability. And the bottom line? The unemployment rate for disabled people was 8.4%, compared to 4.6% of those without a disability.

This has undoubtedly been exacerbated by the pandemic, given that Covid-19 has presented many issues in the workplace. Many disabled employees, who are more likely to be classed as vulnerable to the virus than their non-disabled colleagues, feel their careers have been negatively impacted by having to shield. While some employers went out of their way to enable them to work from home, others just furloughed their disabled members of staff.

Addressing the elephant

You need to be confident about hiring, managing and inspiring people with disabilities. One of the biggest issues to overcome is fear. Employers are often concerned that if a staff member has a disability, they won't be able to performance-manage, discipline or terminate that employee for fear of an employment tribunal (ET) claim for disability discrimination.

The hope is that you manage your staff well and create an environment that means that you never need to defend a claim for disability discrimination, but with 71 ET cases for disability in the year 2019/20 and the highest claim over £265,000, you need be able to defend yourself should the need arise. To defend yourself against such a claim, you will need:

- To be able to demonstrate a positive approach to people with disabilities
- Evidence of proper systems and processes in place across all aspects of your business
- A robust policy on equality, diversity and inclusion (EDI)
- Good EDI training for all staff, including managers on a regular and ongoing basis
- To be able to demonstrate that reasonable adjustments have been made

In addition, in the case of a disabled employee, you may well need communication from their GP and professional reports from an occupational health specialist. This may well be the case if a medical condition emerges or worsens while the employee is with you.

You need to be aware of your company sick pay policy and ensure you stick to it. However sympathetic you may be to a sick employee, you can't treat them differently from the rest of your workforce without opening yourself up to the risk of a claim or signing a blank cheque. This is hard and an issue we have had to discuss with so many clients and their employees. However, it is far easier to stick to your policy and pay someone in line with your sick pay procedures than it is to have to move them on to statutory sick pay four months down the line when they've been diagnosed with cancer.

If you have a concern about someone's health, speak to them. Ask questions such as:

- 'We're concerned about you. We've noticed you holding your arm awkwardly. What's going on?'

- 'We are concerned about you. We've noticed you are becoming very out of breath walking up and down the stairs. What can we do to help you?'

As an employer, you have a duty of care. You must ensure that your staff are safe to carry out the work you need them to do. If in doubt, have a conversation.

Additional information

The UK government runs a scheme called Disability Confident, which encourages employers to hire people with disabilities. By signing up to such a scheme, you access information and support that will assist you with the employment of people with disabilities and position yourself as a socially conscious employer, giving you access to people with skills who sometimes just need a little more support, or even just someone to give them an opportunity.

Disability Confident: disabilityconfident.campaign.gov.uk

Stories from the wild –
Disability and sickness

Over the years, there have been lots of incidents of disability and sickness in the workplace, but for obvious reasons I need to protect the identities of staff and colleagues I have supported.

So let's start with me!

My personal relationship with disability is that I just deal with it and find ways to cope – like thousands of others every day.

I have a genetic disorder called Ehlers Danlos Syndrome Type III, which affects my joints. At 17, I was paralysed and told I would probably never walk again (although they didn't actually know what was wrong with me). I dropped out of school as I had missed so much and, once I was able to, I worked as a receptionist with my dad's employer. Dad drove me to work every day and I walked around the office with a walking stick. Eventually I went back to school and restarted my sixth form. After another year off, I went to university and was a registered disabled student throughout my time there.

Even today, I have issues with my joints and seven years ago had major surgery on my knee. As the orderlies arrived to take me down to the operating theatre that day, my mobile phone rang. It was one of my team who was onsite with a client doing a very challenging sexual harassment investigation in a residential care home. She had been asked to go and see the alleged perpetrator in his house on the client's site and was not comfortable doing so due to the nature of the allegations she was investigating. What could I say? I had two seconds before I was going to be taken down to surgery. How could I support an employee who really needed reassurance? All I could do was tell her to call another member of the team and discuss options. I trusted her to make the right decision and to keep herself safe.

That same wonderful employee drove me to South London two weeks later for a client meeting when a client refused to accept that I couldn't get to see them as I was in plaster from thigh to ankle and they had to see me to discuss an urgent situation. I literally cried when I got there and found an old-fashioned stone staircase leading up to their front door. Giving my bags to my colleague, I carefully used my crutches to get up the stairs without causing myself any further damage.

The smallest room possible

Many years ago, when I was doing a lot of recruiting, I used a couple of meeting rooms on a regular basis. They weren't huge, but they were big enough for four people to sit comfortably. One day, I had eight back-to-back interviews and the normal room was being used by someone else, so I used a very small meeting room that was generally only used for internal one-to-one meetings.

The candidate was a young man in his early 20s and we were chatting about his work experience when he suddenly went quiet, looking up from where I was scribbling notes, I realised that he wasn't ok. Two

43

seconds later he slumped in the chair and started to seize.

I threw open the door of the office and yelled for a colleague to come help me. I had to get the table and chairs out of the room and get the candidate on the floor. My colleagues froze when then saw the fitting candidate, but I started barking orders:

'Sarah, take the chair; Steve, get the table out of here; Jenny, get Michelle out of her meeting and tell her I need her now; Tracey, call the recruitment agency and see if they have next of kin details; Hayley, call 999; Marie, call security and tell them to hold my next candidate down there and that we have an ambulance on the way.'

Meanwhile, I got the candidate out of the chair and onto the floor and then waited for the seizure to pass. It felt like ages, although it all happened very quickly. Our biggest concern was that we knew nothing about this young man. He wasn't an employee; we had no idea if this was his first seizure or a regular occurrence or what his recovery time was.

Fortunately, the paramedics arrived and took the young man to hospital. Following up with the agency, he was ok, but was too embarrassed to continue with his application to work with us.

When 999 doesn't work

This story fortunately had a happy ending, but it could have been so much worse. I'm calling these employees Shelley and Lucy. Lucy reported to me and her mum, Shelley worked in another department.

Lucy went running off out of the office and it was obvious something was wrong. I asked a colleague and was told that Shelley wasn't feeling very well. Being in HR and having dealt with first aid situations for years, I went to investigate.

I found Shelley lying on the floor and everyone crowded around her. She was clutching her head and complaining of a throbbing headache. The department first aider didn't really know what to do and although I was not a qualified 'First Aider at Work', I ended up stepping in. After asking a series of questions and recommended we call 999 immediately. I had a couple of ideas in my head and hoped they were all wrong.

Shelley, Lucy and the First Aider thought I was overreacting and decided that Shelley should be given a cup of tea and then sent home in a taxi. As Shelley started to sit up, she was complaining about the lights in the office. That was it, the bossy HR Manager kicked in again.

'Mary, turn off the lights in this office; Paul, close the blinds; Dave, call 999; Tim, move everyone else up to the canteen, please.'

The lights went out, the blinds were closed, the concerned crowd disbursed but Dave was not happy.

'I can't dial 999, it isn't working.'

'What do you mean it isn't working? Dial 9 for an outside line and then 999,' I responded.

'It doesn't work,' came his panicked response.

'Ok, try it without the first 9,' I suggested.

'Nope,' came the reply.

'Has anyone got a mobile phone?' I asked.

Someone thrust a phone into my hand and I dialled 999. To my relief it worked. Fifteen minutes later the paramedics were with us. I gave them a summary of the situation and, after listening to Shelley who just wanted to go home, to my horror they were going to leave.

I took them aside and shared my thoughts. I believed that she either had meningitis, due to her reaction to light, which they hadn't even asked her about, or that she had an embolism as a result of the pressure in her head. I told them in no uncertain terms that as her employer we were unable to keep her at work and had a duty of care not to put her in a taxi until she had been properly assessed by a neurologist and that they would not be leaving our offices without her. They grudgingly agreed to take her to hospital to get her checked out.

I kept in touch with Lucy over the next couple of days and while Shelley was still in hospital, they couldn't diagnose anything specific except that she had a VERY bad headache. Lucy them told me they were going to discharge her mum and send her back to her GP in a week if the headaches hadn't stopped. I begged Lucy to do everything she could to get a neurologist to see her mum before she was discharged from hospital.

Lucy called me the next day. Shelley was in Queen's Square (Hospital for Neurology) and was having emergency surgery for a brain aneurysm. She made a fantastic recovery, but taught us all two important lessons: one, if you think something is wrong, it probably is; two, use the influence you have to ensure the people you look after are properly looked after.

Shelley eventually returned to work and continued to make a full contribution to her team and the business for a number of years.

Gender/sex

In 2020, with a population in the UK of 67.09 million, 50.6% were female.[8]

With just over half the UK population being classified as female, why are women still having to confront the gender issue in the workplace? A large part of this debate is historical. Until the First World War, very few women worked outside of the home and those who did were generally single and in roles such as nursing or teaching. Today 9.61 million work full time and 5.88 million work part time[9], but there continues to be a large gap in opportunity, progression and pay.

Employers are more willing to accept that women are just as capable as men. In industries and roles where women are still underrepresented, such as engineering, construction and agriculture, there are a variety of initiatives to encourage women to look at companies and roles they would not traditionally have considered.

While many companies are now addressing opportunity and progression, pay remains an issue and many of the issues are focused on the lack of equality in pay. Equal pay legislation was first introduced in 1970. It, like much of the equality legislation was replaced by the Equality Act in 2010, but 11 years later, there are still successful equal pay claims against large employers. Women have won cases in retail and in local government where they have been able to prove that they are paid less than their male counterparts for doing work of equal

---

[8] statista.com/statistics/281240/population-of-the-united-kingdom-uk-by-gender/
[9] UK Parliament Research Briefing – Women and the Economy, March 2021, Brigid Francis Devine, Niamh Foley, Matthew Ward

value. Common comparisons include supermarket staff (mainly female) and their counterparts in the distribution depots (mainly male) and local government where mainly female catering and cleaning staff were paid less than colleagues in male-dominated areas such as street cleaning and refuse collection.

Addressing the elephant

While an increasing number of employers are aware of the gender issues, many don't know how to address the problems in a fair and meaningful way, and the risk of equal pay or discrimination claims must always be a consideration.

Getting the gender issue right from day one is essential and starts at the recruitment stage. Just because the previous job holder was male doesn't mean the next person in the role needs to be male, so when a vacancy opens up, employers really need to review the position, the job description and the attributes needed to be successful in the role. It is healthy for job descriptions to be updated on a regular basis and for a salary benchmarking exercise to be completed before the job is advertised.

Some employers are now advertising blind so that names (as well as indicators of age) are removed from CVs, but this is really not practical in small businesses. While there is a move to video interviews for many businesses, this does pose a risk of bias, so if you are going to use videos as part of your screening process, be very clear about what you are looking for in the video.

Some organisations need to recruit people of a particular gender due to a genuine occupational requirement. If you are going to try to rely on this discrimination exemption, I strongly recommend you take advice before doing so. Increasingly, you will see both male and female attendants in changing rooms in clothing stores or checking toilets in public places.

When promoting employees, open vacancies up to all of your employees by advertising internally for a couple of weeks. Guarantee all applicants an interview and assess performance against clear standards. This gives everyone an equal chance for promotion and career development. One risk with this strategy is if you do not have a good mix of genders further down your company structure, as this could result in a self-perpetuating cycle. If you don't have a good mix of demographics within the business, you may want to think about this when advertising externally for future roles. If you are low on females, advertise in places where females will see your adverts. Think about the wording or the images on your adverts. Make sure you are not putting off applicants because of the way in which you advertise.

I am not an advocate of women-only or men-only shortlists; I do not believe this helps anyone, as the job holder becomes a tick in a statistics exercise. Opportunity, promotion and development should be based on ability, but the employers' challenge is to ensure that they offer the opportunity to everyone capable of achieving, regardless of gender.

Additional information

It's worth remembering that, as with other protected characteristics, discrimination based on sex/gender can be direct or indirect. If an employee is going to take a case against you in the ET (Employment Tribunal), they will always be advised to add in a claim for discrimination on the basis of one of the protected characteristics. The reason for this is that awards for discrimination claims are uncapped.

In 2019/20, there were 46 sex discrimination cases heard by the ET. The maximum award for a sex discrimination case in this period was £73,619, while the average award was £17,420. It is always worth knowing that when a case goes to an ET, it is not the size of the business or their ability to pay that is taken into consideration when making an award, but the nature of the claims and their impact on the employee.

More information can be found on women's equality, pay and discrimination on the following websites:

gov.uk/guidance/work-and-opportunities-for-women

equalityhumanrights.com/en/our-work/equal-pay

equalityhumanrights.com/en/advice-and-guidance/sex-discrimination

Stories from the wild –
Pornography - Building a case file

In order to carry out a disciplinary process on an individual for any misdemeanour, there needs to be a proper investigation. Depending on the circumstances, it may be a short investigation, but potentially an entire file of evidence may be required.

While working for one employer, a senior manager sheepishly approached me and started to discuss some concerns around an employee acting suspiciously. The manager stated that the Peter, the employee was always on his computer, but didn't seem to be getting any work done. Members of the team had complained about missed deadlines and that Peter had been 'acting oddly'.

I agreed with the manager that she would talk to a couple of the team members and encourage them to come and talk to me. Within a week, three employees had been to see me, each with slightly different concerns and examples of Peter's odd behaviour and failure to deliver. I took statements and talked the employees through a potential process we might follow. All the employees were concerned about their anonymity and needed assurances that their statements would be shared with them for sign-off before being provided to the employee concerned, if the situation went that far.

Having got their statements, one thing became apparent: Peter was spending far too much time on his computer, was shutting down his screen when people went past and was making inappropriate comments to some of the female staff members.

I agreed with the line manager that I would pull a computer usage report from IT. Two days later the report came back and a lot of it made no sense. Following a discussion with the IT Director, it was agreed that I would access some of the sites and pull screengrabs as part of our investigation and potential evidence. Having a suspicion about the sites I was about to access, I also got signed approval from my Director and the IT Director to access the sites and store the resulting evidence on my computer!

As expected, they were pornographic websites. I took screengrabs from over 12 sites.

I then wrote to Peter inviting him to an investigation meeting with myself and his line manager. The allegations were of time wasting, accessing non-authorised websites, sexual harassment and storing pornographic material. He attended the meeting with his union representative and was very sure of himself.

I ensured that he knew this was an investigation meeting and that should I believe there was a case to answer, my line manager and his senior line manager would hold a disciplinary meeting. He didn't seem bothered.

I asked if he knew why he was with us and he said no.

I informed him that some of his colleagues were uncomfortable with his behaviour. He stated that he had done nothing wrong and if they were uncomfortable that was their problem.

I went through each of the allegations and he seemed ambivalent, brushing each aside with an excuse.

Eventually, I showed him the report of the websites he had accessed. He tried to claim that this was in his own time, until I pointed out the timestamps. He finally began to look uncomfortable. I then started to show him the screengrabs corresponding to a small sample of the websites. He stopped making excuses and went quiet.

I asked him if he recognised any of the websites and I got no answer.

His union representative asked me to leave the room, which I did, taking his line manager with me.

Five minutes later we were invited back into the room and Peter informed us that he intended to resign with immediate effect.

We checked that this was his union rep's advice, and this was confirmed.

We asked Peter to think about it overnight and if he still wanted to resign to let me have his letter of resignation the next day.

The letter was left at security for my attention the next day. Peter left the building and did not return.

Gender reassignment

It's estimated that 1% of the UK population identifies as transgender or non-binary.[10]

When I first started to see pronoun confirmation ('she/her', for example) in email signatures, LinkedIn profiles and so on a couple of years ago, I thought it was due to the number of international names in the workplace, or to avoid confusion with people who have androgynous names (such as 'Alex', 'Sam' or 'Jess'). Increasingly, it's being used to provide clarity about how people wish to be identified.

Over 20 years ago, my brother came home to tell me how shocked he was that his 'plain' colleague Michael had been leading a double life for years and now, as the stunning Michelle, was completing that transition by coming out at work. 'Coming out' refers to the process that people who are LGBT+ go through as they work to accept their sexual orientation or gender identity and choose to officially disclose to their colleagues and employers.

So, let's use Michelle as an example. As Michael, he was hired and was very capable of doing the job. He was promoted and managed a team of people who respected him for his skill and expertise. Does the view of managers and colleagues change when Michael becomes Michelle? After all, Michelle's skills and experience are precisely the same as Michael's. Her ability to interact with and manage her staff doesn't change. But is her career path the same as it would have been as Michael?

Unfortunately, experience tells us it probably won't be. People who are proposing to transition, actively transitioning,

---

[10] stonewall.org.uk/truth-about-trans

or have transitioned find it hard to be accepted into many workplaces. Their colleagues are still looking for 'Michael' and can feel disorientated. Management is often embarrassed and don't know how to react to the 'newcomer'.

Neither is this a problem only with male-to-female transition. There are reports of people transitioning from female-to-male having the same sorts of experiences and not being able to climb the career ladder, as managers still see them as female and discriminate against them: and all this despite the fact that sex, sexual orientation and gender reassignment are all protected characteristics under The Equality Act 2010.

The sorts of issues HR teams often have to deal with include bullying and harassment, alongside practical issues such as which toilets the transitioning employee should use and which uniform or dress code they should adopt. (In a nutshell, these should be appropriate for the gender as which they identify.) Data protection is also a hot topic; care should be taken to update name and gender data for a trans employee, remembering that it's an offence to disclose someone is trans without their express permission.

Addressing the elephant

To negotiate the evolving world of gender and gender identity, employers need to be actively and frequently reviewing a range of policies and frameworks, including recruitment, pay, promotion, equality, harassment and bullying. Are people being treated fairly, regardless of their gender? Do people compete on a level playing field, irrespective of their gender? Can women earn as much as men and sit side by side at the boardroom table, not in some tokenistic gesture but because they have earned the right to be there?

Additional information

While 'gender reassignment' is the language used in the Equality Act 2010, this wording implies a surgical transition, which many trans people choose not to undergo. 'Gender transitioning' is the process of changing one's gender presentation or sex characteristics to match with one's internal identification. When an employee comes out as trans, their name and pronouns should be confirmed with them and respected. Failure to do so, or for other employees to purposely avoid using them can legally be classed as harassment or discrimination.

As a result of case law in September 2020, individuals identifying as non-binary or gender fluid are now protected under the Equality Act. Jaguar Land Rover did not afford their now female employee the protections she should have been given. On this basis, it makes sense for any responsible business to be supportive and inclusive of all its employees, regardless of gender identity and even if the particular characteristic is not explicitly protected by the Act.

Stonewall: stonewall.org.uk

Equality and Human Rights Commission: equalityhumanrights.com

Sexual orientation

In 2018, 1.2 million people in the UK identified as LGB.[11]

Someone's sexual orientation should not determine their ability to do their job well, to excel in their career and to rise through the ranks within an organisation, yet today there is still a fight for a safe working environment for those from the LGBT+ community. Discrimination, bullying and harassment is still present in the workplace, while prejudices and presumptions are still ingrained in corporate culture. I have it on good authority from friends within the community that life is getting easier, but there is still a long way to go.

For some, sexuality is not something to be discussed in public, regardless of whether you are straight or otherwise. However, for some, coming out has enabled others to feel empowered to do so.

Until 1967, being gay was illegal in the UK. Many homosexuals hid their sexuality for their own safety and for the safety of their friends and loved ones. Today, thankfully, this is not the case, but that doesn't mean that members of the LGBT+ community have full equality of opportunity and are able to work in an environment free from discrimination and harassment.

In some professions it is widely accepted that sexual orientation is less of an issue. If you look on Wikipedia, there are over 200 pages of gay entertainers, including some of my favourites, Sir Ian McKellen, Elton John and Freddy Mercury. In the world of sport, it has taken a lot longer for gay sports personalities to be open about their sexuality. Gareth Thomas

---

11.ons.gov.uk/peoplepopulationandcommunity/culturalidentity/sexuality/bulletins/sexualidentityuk/2018

is a Welsh Rugby Union player who came out in 2009. In 2015, Keegan Hirst became the first British Rugby League player to come out as gay. The time taken between the two public disclosures was a disappointing six years. Interestingly, tennis has been much more accepting of members of the LGBT+ community, with household names such as Billie Jean King, Martina Navratilova and Casey Dellacqua all identifying as lesbians. In the world of fashion, there are a lot of high-profile gay men in the industry including Marc Jacobs, Jasper Conran and Jean Paul Gaultier.

Addressing the elephant

All the same protections afforded to the other protected characteristics apply equally to someone's sexuality. An employer and other staff members are not allowed to treat people differently because of their sexuality. They must be given the same opportunities as all other members of staff and protected from bullying, harassment and discrimination. Employers must ensure that they create an environment in which members of the LGBT+ community feel safe and valued.

It is essential that employers lead by example and create a culture of acceptance with a zero-tolerance approach to any breaches in their equality and diversity policies. It is important that people are trained appropriately and understand the language that should and should not be used. It is vital that where people have concerns these are addressed.

For some, the whole concept of LGBT+ is unacceptable. This is usually, but not always, amongst the very religious of all faiths. These people have rights, too, and they have the right to have their religion and beliefs protected. Therein lies a challenge for employers. If the business has a culture that is open and safe for all regardless of their sexuality, what happens if one or more employees is not open and does not believe that homosexuality is appropriate? An employer cannot force these employees to change their opinions and they cannot be ostracised for holding their beliefs. Freedom of religion and beliefs also means having the freedom to be open about individual beliefs. Likewise, LGBT+ employees cannot be forced to hide who they really are or avoid speaking openly about their relationships and beliefs, wear the clothes they feel comfortable in and not have their names or pronouns respected in the same way as a straight person would.

In this situation, the employer has a facilitating role to play and must enable the parties to find a way to work together for the greater good of the business, its clients and its success. The employer must help the relevant employees to understand each other and find a way to work together without fear of bullying, harassment or discrimination, even if they don't agree. As I said in the introduction of this book, 'do not be disagreeable in your disagreement'.

Additional information

Some large organisations have set up support groups for members of the LGBT+ community within their workforce. Examples include Barclays, and MI5, which was named top employer for LGBT+ equality.

Outandequal.org is an organisation that works with employers and employees across the world to provide resources, events and training to help employers achieve diversity and inclusion within their workplaces.

Marriage and civil partnership

The average number of marriages taking place per year has been declining since 1972. In 1972, 480,285 marriages took place; in 2017, this figure was 271,668. From 2014, the figures include same-sex marriages.[12]

Let's start by understanding the terminology here, as it has changed more recently than any of the other protected characteristics.

Marriage is a union between two people, either a man and a woman or a same-sex couple.

Alternatively, couples, both same-sex and opposite-sex, can enter into a legal arrangement called a civil partnership, which affords them many of the same protections and responsibilities as married couples, including financial, family, medical and inheritance.

In the workplace, anyone who is married or in a civil partnership is protected from discrimination on the basis of their married or civil partnership status.

Unlike other protected characteristics, protection from harassment on the basis of your marital and civil partnership status does not apply. However, the protections from direct and indirect discrimination and victimisation do apply.

Addressing the elephant

This is a relatively rare form of discrimination to the extent that I can't find any statistics relating to ET claims on the basis of marital or civil partnership status. However, that doesn't

---

[12] statista.com/statistics/281533/number-of-marriages-in-the-united-kingdom-uk/

give employers the green light to treat people unfairly. My suspicion is that because a large proportion of the workforce is married or in a civil partnership, those who are harassed or bullied as a result will use one of the other protected characteristics to bring a claim.

As an employer, you must play Inspector Clouseau!

In any situation where someone feels that they are being treated less favourably or in a way that makes them feel uncomfortable, you need to understand why, tactfully and carefully. What else is going on? Is there any form of bullying and/or harassment, even if it isn't on the basis of marital or civil partnership status?

If a woman, when she gets married, is moved from a job that involves working evenings to one that does not, this could be discrimination. If the woman (or man) requests such a change, then that is of course permitted, but you do not have to automatically accept their request if it is not suitable for the business. Likewise, if a man who travels a lot is removed from a role as a result of his new marital status, he, too, might have a claim for direct discrimination.

Communication and consistency are going to be key here. Ensuring that all staff are fairly treated regardless of their marital or civil partnership status must be enshrined in all policies and procedures. If you make a business decision about someone, whether it is hiring, promoting, training or firing, ensure you can back it up based on performance, statistics and objective criteria.

There are very few situations in which an employer could discriminate against someone on the basis of their marital status. One such example would be a community hiring a Catholic Priest. The community would be able to stipulate that the successful applicant must be single, thus discounting applications from any married applicants, therefore directly discriminating against these candidates – should there be any.

Additional information

People living together (not married or in a civil partnership) and single people are not covered by the protections discussed above. There is no concept of being discriminated against because you are single.

There is a good comparison of the similarities and differences between marriage and civil partnerships available from Citizens Advice. As an employer, you may be required to signpost staff to advice and support, but it is important that you don't provide advice based on instinct and what you feel is right. Always ensure your team get the best advice available to them to enable them to make good decisions.

Citizens Advice: citizensadvice.org.uk/family/living-together-marriage-and-civil-partnership/living-together-and-marriage-legal-differences/

Pregnancy and maternity

In 2019, there were 640,370 births in the UK.[13]

Being pregnant is an exciting time for many people, but there is often anxiety around how and when to talk to the employer to tell them about the pregnancy. In many cases this will come down to the type of culture which exists within the business, how previous pregnant employees have been treated and the nature of the relationship between manager and employee.

I recently saw a heartfelt thank you on LinkedIn. In some ways I was really pleased to see how much this senior male executive had felt supported by the business when he took adoption leave, but in some ways I felt disappointed that he was surprised by the amount of support he had and that he felt the need to say thank you and to encourage other males to take advantage of the statutory and company benefits and policies.

There are lots – and I really do mean lots – of legislation around pregnancy, maternity leave, maternity pay, paternity leave, paternity pay, parental leave, shared parental leave, adoption leave, surrogacy and same-sex partners. As you will gather from this list, there are statutory provisions (i.e. those things you must – and must not – do) and company provisions (i.e. things your business does above and beyond the statutory requirements). Not only does this list include pay (including pay rises, bonus and commission) and leave, but also health and safety, time off for antenatal appointments, time off for parenting classes, and rules around sickness, redundancy, 'keeping in touch' days, annual leave, termination and discrimination.

---

[13] ons.gov.uk/peoplepopulationandcommunity/birthsdeathsandmarriages/live births/bulletins/birthsummarytablesenglandandwales/2019

Addressing the elephant

Being pregnant or on maternity leave affords employees a lot of protection and it is essential that, if an employee comes to you and announces that they are pregnant, you don't panic and you do congratulate them. I have had more than one client over the years call me in a panic and inform me that the first word out of their mouth when someone announced that they are pregnant was, 'Shit!' This is not the best start to an open and supportive pregnancy journey. Start by asking them how they feel and when they are due.

If you have never dealt with a pregnant employee before, admit it and tell them that they have your full support, but it will be a learning process for you both. I've worked with a lot of businesses that don't have policies in place for any pregnancy or maternity related issues until they have their first pregnant employee. Most contracts of employment will confirm that statutory maternity, paternity and adoption legislation applies, but most employers do not understand what this means until they have to go through the process for the first time.

It is important to note that the precedent that you set now doesn't just apply to your favourite employee who is telling you they are pregnant, but also to all future pregnant employees as well, or you risk future discrimination claims. You must treat the 35-year-old employee who has been with you for 15 years the same as the 20-year-old employee who has been with you for one year.

If you are a small business, having a pregnant employee who then goes on maternity leave for up to 12 months feels like an insurmountable, expensive challenge. The things you need to think about include whether you have a statutory pay policy or whether you can afford to pay more. Most employers are able to claim back 92% of Statutory Maternity Pay, so it is worth checking this with your accountant.

It is illegal to terminate someone's employment because they are pregnant or on maternity leave, and therefore an employer needs to think carefully about how to ensure cover within the business. Talk to the employee about their plans and reassure them that their job is safe. You may need them to help train up a temporary replacement; discuss the timing of this with them and involve them in the recruitment process, if practical to do so. If you are recruiting someone to cover the role, you cannot offer them a permanent contract unless the pregnant employee has resigned. Even if they tell you they won't come back after maternity leave, unless you can afford two employees, we strongly recommend that you only offer the maternity cover a fixed-term contract with one month's notice on either side.

Poor performance is often an issue for employers. Very often the employee has been a poor performer for a long time and the manager just hasn't done anything about it. Just because someone is pregnant doesn't mean you can't performance manage them; you just need to ensure you are capability managing them or disciplining them for reasons that are not related to pregnancy.

Anyone on maternity, adoption or shared parental leave is afforded a high level of protection from redundancy. Apart from situations where a business is closing, they should be top of the list for a suitable alternative position and consulted alongside other team members. There is currently a proposal for this protection to extend for up to six months after they return to work, so watch employment legislation for these changes.

'Keeping in touch' days are a formal mechanism for enabling employees on maternity leave to stay in touch with the business. Discuss how and when you will communicate with the employee. You can't expect them to keep an eye on their work emails while they are off, so agree which email or phone numbers they want used. Discuss what they want to be involved in. If you do a team picnic every summer, would they like an invitation? If you do an annual Christmas dinner, would they like the opportunity to attend? While an employee is on maternity leave, they are out of the business, but do have the right to be kept informed.

Additional information

Parental status

In 2019, 75% of mothers and 93% of fathers with dependent children were in work in the UK.[14]

Parental status is not a protected characteristic in its own right (yet). So rather than confuse readers, I have included section as an extension of maternity status. As you will see, there are still some employee rights and protections for working parents, regardless of it not being a recognised 'protected characteristic'.

Being a working parent is hard. For me, it was actually more difficult when my kids were at primary school than in the nursery years. Primary school seemed to operate on the assumption that you could drop off at 8.50am then pop back for a lunchtime concert or the 2pm parent-consultation session at the drop of a hat. At least at nursery there was cover from 7am to 7pm if I needed it.

Of course, some employees can work flexibly from home, completing their contracted hours for the week when it suits them and their families. However, that is not the reality for

---

[14] ons.gov.uk/employmentandlabourmarket/peopleinwork/employmentandemployeetypes/articles/familiesandthelabourmarketengland/2019

most. There is also increasing evidence that men want to be more involved in their children's upbringing. Add to this the trend for more women to return to work when their children are very young, and it's obvious that employers need to take a reasonable, practical and legal approach to accommodate working parents of both genders in order to maximise their potential.

But what options could you make available for working parents in your business?

While parental status is not strictly a protected characteristic, employers are nevertheless obliged to ensure that employees are not treated less favourably as a direct, indirect, or implied response to the fact that they have (or will have) children. Recruitment, promotion, training opportunities, job roles and redundancy must be based on skills, experience and the ability to do the job when compared to colleagues without children.

An employer cannot assume a woman would be unwilling to travel to America on business for four weeks because they have kids. (Neither can a line manager elect someone to work late because they *don't* have kids.) Assumptions are dangerous and can lead to claims of bullying, harassment and discrimination, *even when the employer thought they were doing the right thing.*

One estate agent who was denied a flexible working request that would have enabled her to collect her daughter from nursery was recently awarded £185,000 for indirect sex discrimination. Although she did not have a claim based on her parental status, there was enough evidence to demonstrate that the business behaved in a way which impacted her as a woman more than it did her male colleagues.

Addressing the elephant

All parents have an allowance of 18 weeks unpaid parental leave for each child up to their 18th birthday, which is transferable between employers. A parent can request a maximum of four weeks per child per year, to be taken in whole-week blocks. However, employers don't automatically have to grant it; the timing must be agreed between both parties, especially if it has been requested to coincide with school holidays. Parents cannot be penalised in any way for taking unpaid parental leave and are still entitled to their usual range of benefits, training, annual leave, and career progression. Despite this leave being a statutory entitlement, there is no government monitoring or control of it.

It is important to know who has children or family and who doesn't. This is for many reasons, including building effective professional relationships with your staff, offering the right benefits, giving the best support and, as Covid-19 has shown us, knowing who is trying to balance home working with home schooling.

Stories from the wild –
Pregnant at work

I was very lucky both times I was pregnant at work. I had supportive bosses and although the legislation was quite different back then, my personal motto was, 'I am not ill, I am pregnant,' and for me, life continued pretty much as normal. However, I do have some funny stories!

The Alien

I was doing a lot of interviewing the first time I was pregnant. I was recruiting for two IT vacancies and was interviewing a lot of techie guys. They are not generally known for their interpersonal skills, so you have to get them talking about technology to really get them to open up. One candidate would not make eye contact with me. Not unusual, but he seemed distracted. Following his eyes and the look of horror on his face, I looked down at my stomach to see that my unborn baby's foot was protruding and moving from side to side morphing my stomach as it moved. I instantly understand the distraction, it looked like an alien was about to burst forth from my stomach. I moved my papers and held the recruitment pack over my bump and moved swiftly on to the next question.

A baby under the desk

When that same baby was five months old, I received a phone call from my manager. Could I please, possibly, perhaps, go into the office the next day as the IT and HR Directors had decided I was the best person for a project that would start to implement a company website with interactive recruitment pages. The kick-off meeting was the following day and as I was due back from maternity leave in three weeks' time, would I mind coming in for half a day?

At the time, there was no such thing as a 'keeping in touch' day, so it was unplanned and I had no childcare. My manager said that she would look after my son while I was in the meeting and that it really would be appreciated.

I duly took my sleeping little bundle in his car seat into the office and introduced him to my colleagues for the first time. I then put him into his car seat and he fell asleep, so I left him with my manager and went off for a two-hour meeting.

When I returned to collect him, he was just waking up, so I took him into the staff canteen so that I didn't interrupt people who were working. One of my colleagues asked to have a cuddle and my son promptly threw up all down her back! A manager from the Finance team came in and, seeing my son, asked where he had been while I was in the IT meeting; with my manager I informed him.

'But I was with your manager for an hour; there was no baby in there!'

Turned out my son was tucked away under the desk, fast asleep.

Pregnant on a train

Like many entrepreneurial business owners, I don't often say no. It is a skill I have had to learn and practise, but I did say no to this one!

While working for Metronet, I was made aware of some health and safety concerns in the staff toilets in one of the sidings. I was asked to go and investigate.

'Where do I need to go?'
'But we don't have a depot there!'
'How do I get there?'
'You want me to do what?'
'Have you looked at me?'
'I am 32 weeks pregnant and you want me to sit in a train cab into the sidings and then climb down onto the track, which is about 5ft, to go and look at the state of the toilets?'
'OK, let's think about this practically.'
'Can you bring me some photos? I can then look at the images, talk to the staff concerned and find out what they would like to put in place. If it is practical and solves the problem, we do it. I am not climbing down out of the train cab and then being pushed or hauled back up.'

There was more than one way to crack this nut, and being a nut was not the way to do it.

Race

In the 2011 census, 86% of the population in England and Wales identified as White, 7.5% as Asian/Asian British and 3.3% as Black (African, Caribbean or British).[15]

I often ask myself how, in 2021, race can still be an elephant in the room in the workplace, for both employers and employees. After all, it's over half a century ago since the Race Relations Act first came into force – in 1965, to be precise – and outlawed discrimination in public places on the grounds of colour, race, or ethnic or national origins. It was updated in 1976 and 2000, and replaced by the Equality Act in 2010, yet race is still a cause for concern.

The way quotas are commonly used is a case in point. It's a great idea in principle to have shortlists for people of specific ethnicities or graduate schemes open only to members of the Black, Asian and minority ethnic (BAME) community. However, when employers do this primarily to make their statistics look good, they're doing the right stuff for totally the wrong reason and it can backfire badly.

Everyone wants to feel valued. They want to feel they got the job based on who they are, not because they ticked a box. They want to advance because of merit and proven ability. They want an equal voice, not a privileged voice. They want to see role models and people like them progress, be heard and make a difference.

Discrimination legislation has certainly made employers nervous, but it has also split the BAME community.

---

[15]ons.gov.uk/peoplepopulationandcommunity/culturalidentity/ethnicity/articles/ethnicityandnationalidentityinenglandandwales/2012-12-11

Years ago, I remember asking a lecturer who had been made redundant – along with some 50 colleagues –why she was bringing a tribunal claim for race discrimination. Her answer? 'Because I am a woman of colour; therefore, I can.'

All the affected lecturers were being terminated because their subjects were no longer being offered to students. Race or any other protected characteristic never came into it, so it did feel as if she was detracting from people who had genuine race discrimination claims.

Conversely, I've recently been helping a lady who has been bullied and harassed out of her job. She has a genuine race discrimination claim – and several other legitimate claims, too – but the employer scared her so much she won't bring any. She has chosen to move on, and I can understand why, but it does mean an employer remains unchallenged on its race discriminatory practices.

Addressing the elephant

As an employer, you have a legal responsibility to ensure no one is discriminated against in your workplace, and that means:
- Having a comprehensive EDI policy in place
- Training staff to ensure everything from hiring to firing (and all points in between) is aligned to your EDI policy
- Consulting, involving and educating
- Living your policies – you need to lead by example
- A zero-tolerance approach to harassment, bullying, exclusion or discrimination on the grounds of race

It's about ensuring that everyone feels comfortable at work, able to express their thoughts, ideas and concerns free from harassment, regardless of their race or the race of the colleagues around them.

Additional information

While the terms 'ethnicity' and 'race' are often used interchangeably, race is usually associated with biological and physical characteristics such as skin colour and hair texture, while ethnicity is often linked to how people identify and can be linked to nationality. The list of races for census purposes will vary from country to country and over time as society continues to migrate and evolve.

There are generally five widely accepted races: White, Black, Asian, Polynesian and Native American. Over time, these groups have become less distinct due to migration and interracial relationships.

In 2007, the Equality and Human Rights Commission was set up in the UK to promote and enforce equality legislation across all aspects of society, not just employment.

Equality and Human Rights Commission:
equalityhumanrights.com

Stories from the wild –
How many protected characteristics does it take to become memorable?

Y2K

As slightly older readers may remember, a lot of companies were very concerned about something that became known as Y2K. To briefly explain this, when we and our computers wrote dates, we used two digits for the year. The concern was that as we moved from 1999 to 2000, all computers would crash and the world would come to a grinding halt. As a result, Y2K consultants were setting up all over the place and working with businesses to ensure that all their business systems were robust and that life would continue uninterrupted at one second past midnight on 1st January 2000.

In November 1999, I received a letter from a speculative applicant I had rejected accusing me of being:

- Ageist – the applicant was 55 and had enough experience to do the role
- Racist – his mother was German
- Anti-religion – he was a practising Irish Catholic
- Against IT consultants – he was perfect for our business and I was too I to see it
- Disability discrimination – he had a bad back and required regular rest breaks and an ergonomically designed chair…

You get the idea.

After a couple of seconds of panic and then five minutes of hysterical laughing, I went and found his application. In those days every application was kept in hard copy and every applicant received a written response. I drafted a response and then asked my manager to look over it. I do remember the look on her face, and she asked if I was really going to respond to his nonsense.

Dear xxxx,

Thank you so much for taking the time to apply for a role that does not exist within our IT team. As I am sure you are aware, with just two months to go ahead of Y2K, any sensible organisation would have their preparations done and complete. Although your letter states I am incompetent as I have not hired you, I can assure you our Y2K preparations were complete six months ago and therefore we do not have need of your highly skilled and professional services.

I note the nature of your complaints and would like to assure you that we will defend ourselves against all your allegations fully and robustly.

I would like you to note the following:

- Ageist – as you will note from your application, there is no reference to your age and therefore I have been unable to discriminate against you on this basis
- Racist – please take a look at my surname and rethink your allegations
- Anti-religion – please would you arrange for me to have evidence from your application as to the basis of my decision-making based on your religion

- Against IT consultants – I am married to one, so I don't believe your argument would hold up in an employment tribunal
- Disability discrimination – if required I will make my personal medical history available to your legal representative

I have now passed your application, letter of complaint and a copy of this response to our legal team who are eagerly awaiting your employment tribunal claim. They can be contacted on xxxx, should you have any further queries.

Thank you for your interest in our company and for wasting my time in such an entertaining way.

Yours sincerely,

Donna Obstfeld
HR Manager

I don't usually advocate taking this approach to such serious allegations and would not do so myself these days, but in 1999 with different employment legislation and Y2K well and truly under control, I just couldn't resist.

Religion or belief

'Never discuss politics or religion in polite company.' Anon

Unless you are working for a religious organisation, there are unlikely to be circumstances under which you can discriminate against people based on their religion and/or belief. Within most religious organisations, it may be that being of the same faith is irrelevant to being able to do a job for that organisation. Does a receptionist, marketing assistant, financial controller or security guard need to be the same religion as the organisation in which they are working? Generally not.

If there is a need to recruit or promote someone who is of the same religion as the community the organisation serves, then there must be an objective, defendable and genuine occupational requirement. An example of this would include a priest for a church, a Hindu teacher for Hindu lessons in a school or a Jewish person to work as a Mashgiach (the person who certifies food as kosher).

It is important to be aware, that an employee does not need to have a religion or specific belief in order to claim discrimination if they believe they are being discriminated against for lack of a religion or belief.

A belief can be religious or philosophical and must affect the way in which the employee lives their life. It must be more than just an opinion. Examples which have been presented in the ET include being vegetarian, the belief that biological sex (the sex assigned at birth, usually based on X and Y Chromosomes) is different from gender identity and the belief in anti-hunting (fox and hare). There are lots of examples where an employee has tried to argue that a certain behaviour or attitude is a belief and therefore protected, but the criteria are very stringent, so any case would be twofold. First, is the behaviour and / or opinion a protected belief? Second, was discrimination, harassment etc a result of the belief?

Addressing the elephant

Religion and belief are always very sensitive areas that can cause a lot of conflict in society, never mind the workplace. Most global conflicts are about religion and land and these have a bad habit of overflowing into the workplace.

Multiracial, multicultural workplaces with strong EDI practices are often some of the more robust, more successful organisations, as employees draw on their differences and employers effectively use those differences to help drive the business forward. However, those differences can also be the cause of minor disagreements or major arguments. After 9/11, some of the Muslim employees within our business struggled as they sought to try to distance themselves from the terrorists who had killed seven of our colleagues. They felt the need to explain and defend Islam as a peaceful religion and to condemn the fanaticism that had led to the destruction of the Twin Towers in New York.

There are lots of ways in which employers can help create an open an accepting culture, and, of course, discussion and education promote greater understanding and tolerance. There are also traditions that can be shared and food often plays a central part in religious festivals. Encouraging employees to share food at particular times of the year can be a really powerful way to promote harmony and acceptance.

Company dress codes can also be sensitive issues for employees of different religions and beliefs. As far as possible, we encourage employers to have policies that respect the dress codes of all employees. Whether it is a policy that requires

Jewish women to be modestly dressed, allows Sikh men to wear their turbans or permits Christians to wear a crucifix, unless there is an absolutely essential reason for prohibiting religious freedom through dress, your company dress code needs to be flexible enough to meet the needs of the business and the needs of your staff. One mistakes that employers often make is developing a policy that is then applied to everyone. They naively think that in having a standard policy that applies to everyone, they are being fair and therefore non-discriminatory. It is often these employers who end up fighting big legal cases because they haven't taken into account individual needs and are therefore discriminating against people, either directly or indirectly as a result of their standard policy.

There are going to be some exceptions. One example might be a Muslim woman in a full burka. It would be very hard for her to work in a community of deaf people who need to be able to lip read, but, depending on her specific job, not impossible. Employers must ensure that they take all reasonable steps to accommodate the needs of their staff and their potential staff; it is possible for someone to bring a claim if they believe they have been discriminated against in the recruitment process.

The need for regular prayer is another area that employers should be aware of. Jews and Muslims have specific times of the day or week when they are instructed to pray, and many public body organisations now have specific prayer rooms or space set aside for prayer. Allowing people to be flexible with their breaks or their working hours may be sufficient to facilitate prayer among those who wish to pray. I don't encourage employers to give extra breaks or to reduce hours (although these are options that can be individually negotiated), but rather to enable flexibility. An example of this might be shorter lunch breaks during the week to enable a Muslim to attend Friday prayers; or a change in working hours in the winter months to enable a Jew to leave early on a Friday.

As with all things people related, open communication and discussion is essential. Understanding what people want and need and then working together to figure out how to make that happen without detriment to the business is essential. In many cases, employees will have dealt with the issues before or have friends in employment elsewhere who have put arrangements in place. The key is to be open minded and to engage to establish a win-win. Employers who dig their heels in and refuse to even engage in conversations about reasonable adjustments for those with specific religious needs are not going to be able to defend themselves in an ET, and it will take its toll on the business if the employee brings a claim.

When the laws around equality of belief came into effect in 2010, there was discussion about seemingly more trivial matters such as football teams. The rivalry between fans and the belief that one club or national team is better than another is very real and, in some environments, can lead to some very hostile behaviour, including hooliganism. Employers need to ensure that the loan Arsenal fan in an office of Tottenham supporters is not discriminated against because of their devotion to Arsenal, or the German employee is not vilified when England plays Germany at Wembley.

Although unlikely to be able to bring discrimination or harassment cases under the Equality Act, it doesn't prevent the employee bringing a case for bullying. An employer has a duty of care to protect all employees and to create a working environment that is physically and psychologically safe and that includes from bullying. What some will cast off as 'friendly banter' or 'lads being lads', can lead to employees feeling excluded, side-lined and bullied. This has a negative impact on individual and team performance and can then impact on the business. Employers must ensure that they don't allow people to be bullied because of their beliefs, whether they are protected by the Equality Act or not.

Additional information

According to Wikipedia, it is estimated that there are 4,200 churches, denominations, religious bodies, faith groups, tribes, cultures and movements across the world.

For a belief to be accepted as a protected belief by an ET, it must meet five tests. It must:

1. Be genuinely held
2. Not just be an opinion or viewpoint based on the present state of information available
3. Relate to a weighty and substantial aspect of human life and behaviour
4. Attain a certain level of cogency, seriousness, cohesion and importance
5. Be worthy of respect in a democratic society and not incompatible with human dignity or in conflict with the fundamental rights of others

Through case law we know that Holocaust deniers and those who believe in racial superiority are not protected. We also know that humanists, pacifists, vegetarians and those who are concerned about climate change are protected.

Stories from the wild –
Rehabilitation of offenders

Happiness

Although not a protected characteristic, there are laws against discriminating against someone because of their criminal record. These are complex and extreme care must be taken, but on one such occasion, I caught this ex-criminal red-handed…

I spent a lot of my early career recruiting as the businesses I worked for were growing. As a result, I became quite a tough interviewer and, with my degree in psychology, really liked to understand the candidate, what drove them and whether they would be the right fit for our business. I saw lots of people who could do the job, but the right people had to be the right fit!

I don't remember what role I was recruiting for, but I do remember the candidate. His CV was impressive, but there was something wrong. There were a couple of gaps I wasn't happy with and I didn't feel the explanations he was giving me were honest; but they were plausible, so I moved on, but with a niggle I was listening to.

The candidate then went on to discuss a project he had been involved with and it was a study into happiness. He explained the details well and told me the part he had played in the study. He answered all my questions confidently, but then my niggle yelled in the back of my head.

My next question was, 'So could you please tell me which prison you were detained in at the time you participated in the study?'

His face went white, then red. He couldn't get his words out. He spluttered. He coughed. He looked down at his feet and eventually in a very quiet voice asked how I knew he had been in prison. Unfortunately for this candidate, I was a student of Psychologist Professor Richard Wiseman at the University of Hertfordshire and this was one of his research studies that we had learnt about while at university. The study was conducted on prisoners and therefore the gaps in his CV that I was uncomfortable with were because he was detained at Her Majesty's pleasure.

I asked him if he knew about the Rehabilitation of Offenders Act and he informed me his conviction was not spent. He then stood up and informed me his interview was over. I asked him to sit down and listen to me.

While I agreed he was not my ideal candidate, I offered him some advice: don't lie!

Have a chat with your recruitment agencies and be frank with them. Tell them what happened, when and why. It was the dishonesty that cost him this job, not the gaps on his CV, his skills, or the fact that he had served time. I advised him to find a way to address the issue and face it head on, as the right employer would accept him with his background and skills.

I have no idea what happened next in that man's life, but if he hadn't lied, life might have been quite different.

MENTAL HEALTH ELEPHANTS

'Life doesn't get easier or more forgiving, we get stronger and more resilient.'
Steve Maraboli

Depression

Depression is the predominant mental health problem worldwide. More women than men report having symptoms of depression.[16]

Depression can affect anyone. It's the most common mental health condition in the UK – and, indeed, the world.

Most people go through periods of feeling down, sad or depressed at different points in their lives, often as a response to situations such as stress, bereavement, relationship breakdown or job loss. In medical terms, depression is diagnosed when someone's low mood becomes overwhelming and persistently and adversely affects their daily life for two weeks or more.

Symptoms of clinical depression that you as an employer might notice include:

- Avoiding contact with colleagues
- Struggling with their regular workload
- Decreased productivity
- Problems concentrating or making decisions
- Moving or speaking more slowly than usual
- Being tearful in the office
- Lack of cooperation
- Absenteeism or presenteeism
- Complaints about them from colleagues
- Complaints from them about everything

---

[16] mentalhealth.org.uk/statistics

Addressing the elephant

If you think an employee could have depression, you have a duty of care towards them, but you aren't there to solve their mental health issues. Your remit is to agree a plan and discuss how they want you to support them.

First, you need to identify the appropriate person to broach the subject. This may be their line manager or perhaps someone from HR. If your business has a mental health first aider – someone who's completed a recognised course and gained an understanding of depression as part of their training – I'd recommend speaking to them first about your concerns and then deciding how best to talk to the employee in question.

When you do so, find an appropriate time and confidential space to assess the situation by asking questions and noting their responses. It's imperative not to judge or make assumptions. Seek to understand. One of the easiest ways to start the conversation is to pick up on something that's happened very recently. Don't wait days or weeks to say, 'Do you remember when *XYZ* happened?'

If the employee has been diagnosed with clinical depression, ask if they're getting the right medical support. It's acceptable to ask if they are on medication. You may feel it beneficial to suggest they go back to their GP or mental health team for reassessment if they've not had contact for some time – which may have been the case throughout the pandemic. If they aren't getting medical support, you could help them explore the options for obtaining it.

Additional information

Under the Equality Act 2010, a mental health condition is treated as a disability if it has a long-term effect (lasting or likely to last 12 months) on normal day-to-day activities (such as using a computer). If this is the case for an employee who has been diagnosed with depression, then an employer must make reasonable adjustments to enable them to continue working. This might include time off for therapy or offering flexible working hours.

GOV.UK:gov.uk/when-mental-health-condition-becomes-disability

NHS: nhs.uk/mental-health/conditions/clinical-depression/

Mental Health First Aid (England): mhfaengland.org

Anxiety

Between 3.3% and 7% of the UK population will develop an animal phobia at some point in their life, and around 2% have a panic disorder.[17]

Anxiety can be a good thing, helping us avoid dangerous situations and motivating us to solve problems. However, at the other end of the spectrum, it can be utterly debilitating. Anxiety disorders include generalised anxiety disorder, panic disorder, phobic disorder, post-traumatic stress disorder (PTSD) and obsessive-compulsive disorder.

Anxiety manifests in different ways for different people and may vary over time for the same individual, but in general the symptoms can be roughly grouped into three types:

- Physical – including chest pains, hyperventilation, sweating, headaches and muscles aches
- Psychological – decreased concentration, difficulty making decisions, tiredness, intrusive thoughts
- Behavioural – avoidance of situations, repetitive compulsive behaviour, distress in social situations

In some cases, it may be easy to spot a problem. I've had cynophobia – fear of dogs – since childhood, despite all sorts of attempts to cure me. At one point I worked in an office that seemed to be full of dogs. My heart would race, I'd become sweaty, agitated and distracted – even writing about this now, many years later, is making me feel distinctly uneasy. As you can imagine, it wasn't difficult for me or any of my co-workers to see my anxiety and what was causing it. With other people, however, their anxiety may be harder to spot and at work may

---

[17] Adult MHFA Manual, MHFA England, 2016 pg. 181

manifest itself less directly, perhaps as poor performance or high absence rates.

Addressing the elephant

Anxiety is regarded as a disability when it's affecting an employee's performance at work, so your role is to be supportive and understanding, rather than go down the disciplinary route, which, sadly, is so often the kneejerk reaction.

Broaching the subject and discussing concerns sensitively is essential, so ask open questions and listen carefully to what is being said; it helps to summarise, paraphrase and confirm the points raised. The person may have a diagnosis or may not even realise there is a problem. They may be on medication or they may have refused help. When you start the conversation, you have no idea what you are walking into.

As an employer, you have a duty of care towards all your staff and a legal obligation to ensure they are working in an environment free from physical and psychological risks. All employers must carry out risk assessments for their businesses and employees working from home, including physical and psychological factors. You need to understand if your employees are anxious about any aspect of their working life or whether it's being affected by external anxieties.

Finally, a small but important tip: don't invite someone who has anxiety issues for a meeting without saying what it's for. Sending a quick 'Are you free for a chat this afternoon?' message is virtually guaranteed to stoke anxiety. Being clear and open in all your communications is invariably the best approach.

Additional information

Some types of mental health conditions, including anxiety, can be classed as a disability under the Equality Act 2010 if they have a long-term impact on routine activities. If this is the case, the employer must make reasonable adjustments to accommodate the affected staff members' needs. This might include providing a quiet space for them to work in.

There are effective treatments available to help people with anxiety disorders have a better quality of life, but many don't realise this and therefore don't ask for help.

NHS:nhs.uk/mental-health/conditions/generalised-anxiety-disorder/

GOV.UK:gov.uk/when-mental-health-condition-becomes-disability

Anxiety UK: anxietyuk.org.uk

No Panic: nopanic.org.uk

Stories from the wild –
Phobia and panic attacks

While my cynophobia doesn't have a massive impact on me at work, there have been a number of occasions when I and my colleagues have had to deal with the aftermath of an attack. I share these now to help you understand how something so 'normal' can be a problem for you in your business and you need to actively think about how you would deal with the problem if it happened to you. Being able to think things through and plan for it in advance, is half the battle won, but be aware: no plan survives first contact.

The station dog

This story again goes back to my time at Metronet. I'd finished a shift and was heading back home from Edgware Road station. I'd been doing the journey for a couple of months and it was a pretty easy, uneventful journey for me.
One evening, I arrived at the station to discover the drugs dogs were on duty. With their handlers, there were three of them walking around the ticket office and concourse. I hadn't expected them to be there, I didn't know it was a thing and I panicked as the dogs came towards me.
Within seconds I had a complete meltdown. I was shaking, my heart was racing, I was in tears and I could barely stand. A member of the station team came over

to me and tried to talk to me, but I couldn't get any words out. I vaguely remember hearing one of the dog handlers saying, 'She's clean.' I guess the dog had done its job and confirmed I wasn't carrying drugs. All I could do was get my staff card out of my pocket. I was quickly taken into the Station Controller's office, given a drink and a biscuit, and eventually I calmed down enough to tell them what had happened. I called my husband at their suggestion and they called my local station. I could barely walk, but they got me onto the train and my husband met me at the other end and got me off.

My staff card had saved, me, but I always went into the station half expecting to see the dogs again and when I did, I was a little more prepared and as a result, I was able to control myself in that situation a little better. The panic still started to build, but I could talk myself through it and reason with myself until I was safely on the platform and away from danger. The panic doesn't go away, but being prepared and having a plan, means that the response was not a full-blown panic attack.

The prison dog

In 2004, I was working in a prison in Milton Keynes. It was a new build and didn't yet have inmates. There was a lot of recruitment and training to be done and a lot of organising to be put in place.

Although this was a prison for 10–17 year-olds, otherwise known as a secure training centre, drugs were still expected to be a problem and therefore there was a drugs dog and handler on the core team. I knew about this; I'd had a discussion with the Governor about my phobia and I'd had a chat with the dog handler. I'd agreed, in writing, that when required, I would be searched and that it might include my locker, bag, office as well as my person. No problem. I had nothing to hide, I just didn't want to have to deal with another dog incident at work.

One morning I arrived at work and headed through the security checkpoint. After x-raying my bag and walking through the security machine, I entered the airlock. The minute I did, I saw the panic on the dog handler's face. I turned around and I was in the airlock with the drugs dog and had 30 seconds before they could open the door. My body went into immediate panic and shut down. By the time they could get the door open, two of the senior team were waiting for me, the dog handler grabbed the dog and they hauled me off the floor and out of the airlock to enable the rest of my colleagues to be security checked and screened on arrival at work. The dog handler was furious with himself. I had inadvertently tested their systems and he had slipped up. There should have been a sign at the x-ray machine advising people that the drugs dog was on duty, but there wasn't. He had forgotten the sign and the result was an HR Manager in a complete state of shock.

For me it was a terrible day. When your body has had a proper panic attack, all sorts of chemicals are released. I was tearful the entire day, I was shaking, I was shivering and could not get warm. The team decided that I needed to go home but was not safe to drive the 40+ miles to get there. They went out to the nearest petrol station and bought me two large bars of chocolate – for purely medicinal purposes I assure you! I got no work done that day. By 4pm, I had enough composure to drive home safely. I went home and, despite having two young children, went straight to bed.

Lesson to businesses here: if you have a procedure in place, it is probably there for a good reason so make sure you follow it. The dog handler got a lesson in reality that day.

The office dog

As you might imagine, Take Your Dog to Work Day is my greatest nightmare. While I understand that for some people dogs have a calming influence and can be seen as therapeutic, for others, like me, they create the exact opposite effect.

Before you introduce a policy of dogs in the office or even a one-off Take Your Dog to Work Day, you need to carry out a risk assessment. You also need to think about new starters who may not join or who may leave your business with such a policy in place. With the increase in dog ownership as a result of Covid-19 and lockdown, there is going to be an increase in pressure on from employees wanting to bring their dogs into the office. You need to take a decision about how you handle this, document it and communicate it.

Knowing I had a dog phobia, my staff know that dogs are not permitted in our offices. Not only am I not comfortable around dogs, but also there is not sufficient space or facilities for them. On one occasion I was not scheduled to be in the office but dropped in to collect some papers. I was less than pleased to find that one of the team had bought their dog into the office. She was embarrassed and I was furious at the breach and subsequent waste of time. I had to wait for her to take the dog out and put it in the car before I could go in. I also told her to take the dog home and clean up the office before I came back. If I'd had a bigger attack, my day would have been a wipe-out and I would have let down a client.

Self-harm

On average, females are 1.5 times more likely to self-harm than males. The UK has the highest self-harm rate in Europe.[18]

Self-harm is widely misunderstood and one of the most stigmatised mental health issues. While the signs – such as healed scars, open wounds or burn marks – can be visible to others, leading to the erroneous belief that it's about attention seeking, nothing could be further from the truth. People self-harm in an attempt to escape from and manage emotional pain and distress.

Cutting is the most common way to self-harm, but it can also involve burning, hair pulling, head banging, risk-taking (such as walking into traffic), abusing drugs and alcohol, or overdosing. There's also a link with eating disorders such as bulimia nervosa. Contrary to popular belief, self-harm is not intended to be fatal, but those who do it are at increased risk of suicide, often because the stress triggers are the same.

Addressing the elephant

As a work colleague, you need to be understanding, supportive and non-judgemental. You cannot stop someone self-harming. It's not your job to stop them self-harming. Your role is to support them so they feel valued and safe in their workplace.

Mental health first aiders are trained in a five-step approach known as ALGEE:

- Approach the person, assess and assist with any crisis

---

[18] Adult MHFA Manual, MHFA England, 2016 pg. 183

- Listen and communicate non-judgementally
- Give support and information
- Encourage them to get appropriate professional help
- Encourage other support

Each of these stages takes knowledge, practice and skill, but the reality is that the first time you need to use ALGEE is when you're dealing with an actual situation.

If you're going to be of any use to someone who is self-harming, you need to master your own behaviours and control yourself, your emotions and your fears. Give them space to talk and, if they start to open up, be prepared for intense emotion.

Agree an action plan with them. You may offer to do some research into charities who can support them, or encourage them to visit their GP or talk to a mental health specialist. Treatments for self-harm are based on the underlying cause. The individual may need to see a psychologist or undertake a talking therapy such as Cognitive Behavioural Therapy (CBT). They may need medication to control depression or another underlying condition, which may help them stop self-harming.

Additional information

Self-harm appears to affect some groups of people more than others, including veterans, young people, women, members of the LGBT+ community, prisoners, asylum seekers and those who have been abused.

There are a number of services available for people who self-harm, including Harmless, (the national service for self-harm), which also offers support and information to their friends, families and employers.

Harmless: harmless.org.uk

The National Self-Harm Network: nshn.co.uk

Self Injury Support (for women): selfinjurysupport.org.uk

CALM (for men who self-harm): thecalmzone.net

Psychosis

'The neurotic has problems; the psychotic has solutions.'[19]

When someone is experiencing psychosis, their brain misinterprets information, resulting in an altered view of reality that can lead to distress and disruptive behaviour. As you might imagine, it can also be problematic in the working environment, especially as the person experiencing psychosis may not realise anything is wrong with them.

Common types of psychosis include schizophrenia, bipolar disorder and psychotic depression. Symptoms may include hallucinations (including hearing voices and seeing things that aren't there), delusions (such as paranoia), mood swings, withdrawal, expression of unusual beliefs, memory problems or disordered speech. Relationships and self care can also be negatively impacted.

Psychosis can be triggered by a brain injury or tumour, severe trauma, prescribed medication, substance abuse and genetics. Unfortunately, it tends to take a long time to obtain an accurate diagnosis and effective treatment. As symptoms of psychosis often starts in late adolescence or early adulthood, when someone reaches the workplace, they may already have been diagnosed.

Some people with psychosis will be on medication, under the care of expert mental health teams and able to function normally. For their colleagues, problems may only occur if a psychotic episode is triggered, which could be due to an

---

[19] *Thomas Szasz, Hungarian-American psychiatrist*

incident at work or home, a change in medication or because they have stopped taking their medication for some reason.

Addressing the elephant

Every situation will be different, so it's important to assess each one individually and seek advice if you're unsure how to best support your colleague. They may already have an agreed action plan with their line manager or HR. You may have an occupational health report with a strategy in place. You may also need to contact their next of kin to get advice and support.

Whatever you do, don't ignore the problem. It will not go away on its own. You have a duty of care to protect the physical and psychological wellbeing of yourself and your colleagues and, as with all first aid situations, if you can't control the risk your role is to find someone who can.

One thing to be aware of is that, although rare, psychosis can manifest as aggressive behaviour. If this is the case, you must protect yourself and others before assisting the individual. Stay calm and don't try to reason with them – it won't work. Express empathy and, where appropriate to do so, comply with their requests. You may need to call the police and explain that the person has mental health issues including psychosis.

As with all mental health conditions, your job is not to cure the individual. You are there to support them, to protect them if required and ensure that others are safe. If you have anyone else at work with a mental health issue, witnessing a psychotic episode may trigger them in turn, so it's a good idea to do a debrief afterwards and ensure everyone involved is ok.

Additional information

While drug treatment for psychosis is available and generally effective, they can cause unpleasant side effects in some people. CBT is recommended as a treatment for psychotic disorders, and aerobic exercise can help to improve outcomes for people with psychosis.

There are a number of specialist agencies for treating particular psychoses, such as postnatal (also known as postpartum), and for young people. Organisations such as Mind, Rethink Mental Illness and Sane provide help, support and information to those affected by psychosis and other mental health disorders.

The Hearing Voices Network (HVN): hearing-voices.org

Bipolar UK: bipolaruk.org

National Paranoia Network: nationalparanoianetwork.org

Mind: mind.org.uk

Rethink Mental Illness: rethink.org

Sane: sane.org.uk

Suicide

Suicide is a permanent solution to a temporary problem. In 2019, there were 5,691 completed suicides in England and Wales, an average of 19 every day.[20]

Suicide is a complex issue, and one that few people are comfortable talking about. When it involves a colleague, contractor, client or an employee's relative or friend, the impact can be far-reaching, both for team members as individuals, and the business as a whole.

There are a lot of myths surrounding suicide, the biggest being that when someone is feeling suicidal, there is nothing anyone can do or say to make them change their mind. This is not the case. Suicidal thoughts arise when someone can't envisage any other way of dealing with their situation. This may be depression, overwhelming emotional pain, or a particular situation they find themselves in and can't see 'any other way out'. The right help and support will enable them to think more clearly and explore alternative solutions.

Warning signs of potentially suicidal thoughts in an individual may include:

- Withdrawing from others
- Reckless behaviour, including increased use of alcohol or drugs
- Disclosing feelings of anxiety, hopelessness, being trapped or having no reason to live
- An expression of intent to hurt or kill themselves
- Looking for ways to take their own life

---

[20]ons.gov.uk/peoplepopulationandcommunity/birthsdeathsandmarriages/deaths/bulletins/suicidesintheunitedkingdom/2019registrations

- Talking or writing about death, dying or suicide, or of putting their affairs in order

Each affected individual will behave in their own way and may exhibit more than one, or none of these indicators. Conversely, even when someone is exhibiting one or more of these behaviours, suicide might never have crossed their mind.

Depression is a major risk factor for suicide (although not everyone who is depressed will attempt suicide, and not everyone who attempts suicide will be depressed). As an employer or mental health first aider, it's essential to listen to and support an employee who appears depressed or discloses that they are.

Addressing the elephant

As a responsible employer, you need to be aware of the possibility of a suicide crisis affecting your and prepare a plan to support those who need your help – albeit a plan that, it is to be hoped, you'll never have to use.

When dealing with an employee in a suicidal crisis, rapid intervention is paramount:

- Talk to them and encourage them to talk to you
- Don't leave them on their own
- Ask them about their suicidal thoughts – yes, you can do this. Find out if they have a plan? Do they know when and how they intend to attempt suicide?
- Listen without judgement and put your own preconceptions aside
- Don't make assumptions, patronise or be judgemental
- Be polite and respectful of how they are feeling
- Don't deny their feelings – this is their reality

- Don't try to give advice unless you're appropriately qualified to do so
- Reassure them that help and other options are available
- Encourage them to seek help and, if appropriate, offer to help them get the right assistance
- Keep everyone safe – don't do anything that endangers yourself or others
- Call for an ambulance or police intervention if the suicidal crisis is acute
- If you feel the employee is at risk of attempting suicide, get help from a trained professional as quickly as possible. The person may need to be hospitalized until the suicidal crisis has passed.

Additional information

If you need to talk to someone about the issues raised in this chapter, please contact:

Samaritans: 116 123, samaritans.org

CALM: 0800 585858, thecalmzone.net

Stories from the wild –
You've killed me!

'The next time you hear my name will be when the police call you to tell you they have found me in a ditch.'

These were the words yelled at me as one employee left the room. I was shaken and called my dad. Dad had been a Samaritan for over 20 years and was regularly dealing with suicide conversations in a way I, in my short HR career, had never had to. Dad assured me it was unlikely to amount to anything. Unless someone was genuinely suicidal with longer term issues, a one-off incident was highly unlikely to result in a completed suicide. I needed that reassurance, but I was still worried.

I was working for a multinational retailer and one of the field team had been falsifying his work records. Arrival and departure times on site, expenses and significant amounts of time in which the employee was missing in action – it all amounted to fraud. My job was to conduct the disciplinary meeting, present the evidence, obtain his version of the story and to issue a disciplinary outcome.

I had photocopies of the visitor books from stores, I had written statements from store managers, I had copies of parking tickets – he really didn't have a lot he could say in his own defence. He wouldn't explain why he had falsified his records or what he had been doing while he was 'absent from work'. I had no alternative but to terminate his contract by reason of gross misconduct.

His response was an emotional reaction: 'The next time you hear my name will be when the police call you to tell you they have found me in a ditch.'

The worst bit of this was having to escort him to his desk and wait while he cleared it. I then had to escort him down to security and ask him to hand in his security passes before escorting him off the premises.

There are times when being in HR is about helping and supporting people, but this was not one of those times. In this case, my role was to protect the business and to ensure that the employee was treated fairly in line with legislation, policy and procedure.

My Grandma Dora used to run a VG Foods shop. She was always interested in my work and when I tried to explain to her what I did, I tried to use examples I thought she would be able to relate to. Having to conduct an investigation for a disciplinary process made little sense to her.

'Why can't you just fire someone if they have stolen from the business? That's what I did in my day.'

There was a time when if someone stole from you, you fired them and there were no repercussions. That is not the case today. Get it wrong and you could end up in the ET for wrongful or unfair dismissal. Far too many employers get caught out this way. Despite the fact that they may have CCTV evidence or witness statements, they MUST still follow a proper process or they will end up having to compensate the thief.

In 2008, an employee in a flooring company wrote a company cheque to himself for £845. The business owner caught him and marched the employee to the local police station with a sign around his neck that read: 'I am a thief.' The employee then sued his former employer for £90,000 for two years' loss of income, humiliation, distress and PTSD following the incident. In 2011, the business owner paid £13,000 to settle the case outside of court, as to defend himself in court would have cost at least £25,000. In short, he broke the law. As Bananarama and Fun Boy Three say, 'It ain't what you do, it's the way that you do it, and that's what gets results.' In this case, the employer should have gathered the evidence, invited the employee to a meeting and then terminated his employment. This would have been the legal way to fire an employee for gross misconduct and protect the business.

Bereavement

Some 608,002 people are estimated to have died in England and Wales in 2020.[21]

As Benjamin Franklin so wisely said, 'Nothing is certain but death and taxes.'

Unlike some of our other elephants in the room, as an employer you'll have to deal with bereavement impacting your staff at some point, and this has been especially true during the pandemic.

Everyone's experience of bereavement is different. Generally speaking, however, people's reactions will vary depending on who has died:

- An employee or colleague, perhaps from cancer, a car accident or suicide
- Multiple employees and colleagues in a single incident, such as 9/11
- A close relative, such as a partner, child, parent or sibling
- A celebrity such as Diana, Princess of Wales

Whether a death is expected or unexpected will also have a significant influence on how someone copes. Even just hearing about a death can bring back memories and trigger potentially unresolved emotions.

As an employer, you need to be aware of the emotional needs of your staff. After the death of Diana, for example, there was a massive outpouring of emotion and a lot of people felt the need to talk, grieve and express opinions. You can try to push everyone back to work, or you can create a space for people to

---

[21]ons.gov.uk/aboutus/transparencyandgovernance/freedomofinformationfo i/deathsintheukfrom1990to2020

talk. By doing the latter, you enable everyone to move on more quickly and create a culture of openness, respect and support.

Accidents or deaths at work, or of colleagues outside the workplace are the most widely disruptive and likely to have the greatest impact on your staff as a whole. For example, if someone has a fatal heart attack in the office, colleagues who were present may feel guilty for not saving them. In this type of situation, it's advisable to bring in external experts such as bereavement counsellors to provide support and help the business move on effectively.

I know exactly where I was on 9/11. I was working for TK Maxx (TJX). We lost seven members of staff on those planes flying between our head office in Boston to our LA buying office. We had American staff working in the UK and UK staff who got stuck in the US. It was traumatic, but we set up facilities in the canteen and encouraged people to talk, to remember, to share. We held memorial services with our colleagues in the US, and we provided a lot of support through our employee assistance programme. The company had to respond, and we did so quickly.

Addressing the elephant

When a bereavement occurs, and it will, you won't have long in which to decide how to best handle the situation, so it's imperative to have a clearly documented plan for compassionate leave in place.

In April 2020, the UK introduced legislation giving bereaved parents of children up to the age of 18 two weeks of paid leave at the prevailing statutory rate (£151.97 per week as of July 2021). However, there is no statutory pay or leave entitlement for any other type of bereavement, although I suspect it's coming.

When I looked at implementing the new law into my clients' policies, I found most already provided one week of fully paid leave in the event of the death of an immediate family member – usually defined as a parent, sibling, partner or child. In many cases, grandparents or grandchildren were also included. Most have therefore chosen to strengthen what they already offered by adding a second week of leave at the statutory rate.

Whatever you decide on, be consistent and apply it across all areas of your business – and do consider what you would do if you needed to move beyond your policy and provide more leave. From experience, I'd recommend doing so on an unpaid basis, but this will ultimately be a financial and operational decision based on the needs of the business and the individuals involved.

Additional information

While some employees will require bereavement counselling, others will not. Always ensure people know where they can get assistance.

Bereavement Advice Centre: 0800 634 9494, bereavementadvice.org

This is a practical advice line supporting people after the loss of a loved one and will signpost other support services as required.

Grief Encounter: 0808 802 0111, griefencounter.org.uk

One of the biggest challenges for working parents is dealing with the needs of their children after a bereavement. Grief Encounter supports bereaved children and young people.

ABUSIVE ELEPHANTS

'It hurts the most when the person that made you feel so special yesterday makes you feel so unwanted today.'
Anon

Sexual harassment

Some 80% of young women in the UK have been sexually harassed.[22]

As an employer, have you ever assumed any of the following?

- Sexual harassment doesn't exist in your workplace
- As the business owner, you would know if it was an issue
- Everyone is comfortable with the office banter
- Someone being sexually harassed will come forward or others will stick up for them
- The victim of sexual harassment is always a woman, and it's always a man perpetrating it
- Same-sex sexual harassment isn't a problem
- A female manager won't sexually harass a male junior
- Sexual harassment isn't used to exert power
- Sexual harassment will stop on its own
- Sexual harassment is harmless

Sexual harassment is any type of unwanted sexual behaviour that causes distress, humiliation or intimidation. It can involve explicit or suggestive language, jokes, gestures, touch, emails and other communications. Above all, intention is irrelevant; it's how the behaviour is perceived that counts. If someone feels they've been sexually harassed, they have.

Fail to manage sexual harassment and in the eyes of the law you're as bad as the harasser. If the employee brings a claim under the Equality Act 2010, it's possible that the business, you

---

[22] unwomenuk.org/site/wp-content/uploads/2021/03/APPG-UN-Women-Sexual-Harassment-Report_Updated.pdf

as the owner and the perpetrator will all be named as defendants.

Addressing the elephant

As an employer, you have a duty of care towards your employees to ensure your workplace is a safe place, both physically and psychologically – and that means you're obliged to have a zero-tolerance approach to sexual harassment.

Taking these steps will help to achieve this:

- Have a policy stating clearly that sexual harassment will not be tolerated
- Communicate your policy in employment contracts and employee handbooks
- Ensure all new employees are aware of your policy and culture.
- Deliver training to all employees on creating and maintaining an environment that's safe and free from sexual harassment for everyone
- Embed a culture of respect in your business
- Lead by example and don't turn a blind eye for anyone
- Investigate every concern or grievance raised and take appropriate action in line with your disciplinary policy

One final point. If a sexual harassment complaint is made, take it seriously, act on it quickly, and do so fairly, sensitively and openly. Both sides need to be heard.

Additional information

In 2016, the TUC conducted a workplace survey. The report was called *Still just a bit of banter?*, because this was and still is the overwhelming response to allegations of sexual

116

harassment in the workplace. The key results of the survey should be a rude awakening for many employers:

- 52% of women had experienced some form of sexual harassment
- 35% of women had heard sexual comments being about other women in the workplace
- 32% of women had been subject to unwelcome sexual jokes
- 25% of women had experienced unwanted touching
- 10% of women had experienced unwanted attempts to kiss them

Help and support is available from safeline: safeline.org.uk

Domestic abuse

One in four women and one is six men will experience domestic abuse in their lifetime, ranging from coercive control to murder.[23]

There's a widespread perception that domestic abuse (also known as domestic violence) is typically perpetrated by an intimate partner, usually male on female. However, it can affect anyone, including in same-sex relationships. It may be parent on child or child on parent, especially with adult children living at home for longer.

You may assume that someone being abused would have unexplained bruises, scratches or cuts, but not all abuse is physical. Verbal attacks, such as telling someone they are useless, worthless and pathetic, is emotional or psychological abuse. Not allowing someone the freedom to work late, to meet colleagues outside work or to volunteer for a company charity event may be signs of coercive or controlling behaviour. Financial (economic) abuse can involve the employee having no control over their income and not being allowed to spend their money freely.

Statistics suggest one in four women and one in six men experience some type of domestic abuse in their lifetime, and we know this figure has significantly increased as a result of recent lockdowns. It's likely the full extent is not yet known.

Addressing the elephant

While some employers would like to bury their heads in the sand and assume that what goes on in an employee's home is

---

[23]eida.org.uk/s/EIDA-Handbook-v2-July-2021.pdf

nothing to do with their work, this isn't an option. Whether your staff are working from home or in the office, you need to ensure they are safe.

The work environment may be their refuge from their abuser. Look out for signs such as an employee seeming desperate to get back to the office after working from home or being furloughed during lockdown. In this situation, it's worth bringing them in for a chat to dig down into why they want to return. It may be a mental health issue, it may be for a more clearly defined work-life balance, but it may also be to escape to their safe place. Do not hold this conversation online or over the phone. They may not be able to speak or communicate freely if their abuser is present.

You need to be careful not jump to conclusions. One-off incidents may not indicate a problem, but you should have abuse on your radar when dealing with some employees. For example, you may notice changes in a person's behaviour, engagement or performance. Treat these changes in the usual way and have a conversation.

In some cases, the employee may not even realise they are being abused; so ingrained has the abuse become that they accept it as their normal way of life. There will often be other complicating factors, such as finances, family and religion, so you need to tread carefully, but don't shy away from asking questions. Illustrate with examples and ask what you can do to help. If abuse is an issue, you're unlikely to get this as a straight answer, but watch body language, listen to what is being said and, more importantly, to what is not being said.

Additional information

The Employers' Initiative on Domestic Abuse (EIDA) has more information about the employer's role in supporting employees with domestic abuse and domestic violence, and a lot of valuable resources to help you and your managers be better equipped to pick up on potential abuse victims in your workplace.

EIDA: eida.org.uk

Bullying

'No one has ever made himself great by showing how small someone else is.' Irvin Himmel

Do you remember the school bully? If so, why? To misquote Maya Angelou, it's not what they said, but how they made you feel. You might forget the actual words, but you are left with the emotions. This is true whether words are positive or negative, and their impact can be felt for years.

Bullying in the workplace is no different. To assume it doesn't go on is naive. It's more likely to be verbal and behavioural than physical. Calling someone stupid, spreading rumours about them or making disparaging remarks their appearance are all common forms of workplace bullying between colleagues. Bullying from a line manager often manifests itself as micro-management, setting unachievable targets, consistently assigning tasks to the victim that no one else wants, belittling them, denying reasonable holiday requests or making them work late for spurious reasons.

There are many theories about why people bully others, and these often include jealousy, something that has happened to the perpetrator in the past, or their inability to express themselves in any other way. Whatever the cause, workplace bullying is illegal.

As with sexual harassment, the intention to bully is irrelevant; it's perception that matters. A manager may believe they are appropriately managing a poor performer, but to the employee on the receiving end this may feel like bullying. So who is right and who is wrong? This may depend less on what is being done and more on how it's being done. Not everyone is a natural manager, so, as a business owner, you need to ensure your managers have the skills and experience required to get the most from their staff without their team feeling bullied.

Addressing the elephant

Win-wins are rare when you're dealing with allegations of bullying, so it pays to do all you can to minimise the chances of it occurring in the first place. As the saying goes, 'what you permit, you promote. What you allow, you encourage. What you condone, you own.'

Since no employer can have eyes and ears everywhere, you need to foster a culture of zero-tolerance towards bullying and have a policy to underpin it. When staff feel supported and able to report unacceptable incidents, you're less likely to encounter bullying behaviours, not least because no bully wants to get caught.

If a complaint is made, follow your policies and procedures to the letter and carry out a full investigation, including speaking to witnesses and taking statements. Although this process may be long and drawn out, you need the evidence before going to a disciplinary hearing. (It has been known for a manager to face accusations of bullying when in fact it was the direct report who was the bully and manipulating the situation to their advantage.)

It's also important that your investigator is impartial. In a small business, it's sometimes hard to find such a person, so I'd recommend an external investigator, such as an HR consultant, business coach or accountant. Then, if you do end up in an ET, you will be able to demonstrate you've adhered to a fair and robust process.

One of the most effective ways of dealing with accusations of bullying is through mediation. This is best done with an external third-party mediator but may be achievable with a 'let's get everyone round the table' type chat, depending on the circumstances. Bringing people together and inviting them to talk about how behaviours have made them feel is a powerful way of addressing the issue, ensuring the complainant feels supported and the bully understands their behaviour is unacceptable. The aim is to achieve an agreement whereby the two parties are able to work effectively together so that they're both comfortable and effective in their roles.

Additional information

In February 2021, BUPA conducted a survey into workplace bullying. Despite a general increase in wellbeing programmes and a greater emphasis placed on dignity and respect in the workplace, 25% of the 4,000 employees surveyed reported being bullied in the last three years. This figure rose to 33% in the retail sector.

Covid-19 is, in part, believed to have led to the 12% increase on the 2019 report figures, but it is believed that an increase in pressure on employees has led to the increase in bullying. In addition, without being in the same space as colleagues, there is lack of clarity over who to turn to for support and managers don't know how to access support when it is needed. This has enabled bullying to continue under the radar and unchecked.

THE NEW ELEPHANTS ON THE BLOCK

'Magic is when life didn't go as planned, but worked out better anyway.'
Sue Fitzmaurice

Brexit

In 2016, 48.11% voted remain. 51.89% voted leave.[24]

I guess that before I start on this topic, I need to put my cards on the table.

I voted remain, but I could easily have voted leave. I could argue either way depending on whether I was looking at employment legislation, worker migration, holidays in Spain, friends retiring to France, European courts telling us how to run our lives, etc. I completely get why the vote was so close, because the reality was that in some circumstances we would be better off remaining and in others we would experience detriment having done so. Likewise, by leaving the EU and separating ourselves from 40 years of integration, there were pros and cons in every almost every aspect of our lives.

However, this book is about managing people and addressing the elephant in the room that so often occur in businesses. I am going to ignore the arguments and discussions in the workplace during the campaigning and in the days that followed the vote and instead I am going to focus on where we are now.

Addressing the elephant

Depending on what industry you are in, your perspective on Brexit will be very different. In some businesses, there is almost no impact at all. In some businesses, life has become easier, but for some life is certainly still feeling the impact of Brexit.

---

[24]electoralcommission.org.uk/who-we-are-and-what-we-do/elections-and-referendums/past-elections-and-referendums/eu-referendum/results-and-turnout-eu-referendum

While supply chain and logistics remain an issue, the shortage of skilled staff has become one of the biggest issues for many organisations, because of:

- People not willing or able to do certain jobs
- Additional pressure being put on the remaining staff where vacancies exist within business as a result of Brexit
- Staff demanding higher salaries
- Sections of the workforce no longer in the country – this could in part be due to Covid-19, as well
- Sections of the workforce without settled or pre-settled status
- Immigrants from across the world not having the right to work in the UK

In combination, these factors are having a huge impact on employment in the UK. There are 1.2 million vacancies and yet employers are still struggling to find the employees with the right skills and experience.

This elephant isn't necessarily hiding within one organisation, but it is roaming around the entire country causing chaos. Lack of heavy goods vehicle drivers, lack of seasonable fruit and vegetable pickers and lack of carers are just a few examples of the problems being faced. Covid-19 has definitely had an impact on this elephant, but Brexit also has a lot to answer for.

As the job market becomes employee led, businesses must do everything they can to position themselves as an employer of choice. Not only is it important to attract new staff, but also you can't be complacent about your existing staff. You can't hire new staff on higher salaries than your loyal longer serving staff or you will see them walk out the door for higher money.

Employee engagement is going to be essential. Why should people choose to come and work for you? What do your existing employees think of you as an employer? Would they recommend you to their friends and family as the best place to work? If not, why not? That is one great big elephant sitting right there, and you will trip over it if you are not looking carefully and asking the right questions.

Look at your key statistics. How long are people staying? What is the average length of service of your workforce? Do you know, and I mean really know, why each person who has left, has done so? I do recognise that a lot of people were made redundant during the Covid-19 pandemic, but that is in the past (it is hoped) and you can't go on blaming that when Brexit is very much a living reality that will continue to impact on businesses for years to come.

Additional information

The current scheme for Right to Work checks was introduced on 29th February 2008, following on from the introduction of the Immigration Asylum and Nationality Act 2006. Prior to Brexit, it was not necessary for employees from European Countries to have a work permit, but following Brexit and from 1st July 2021, all employees must have settled or pre-settled status or a work permit before they are allowed to work in the UK.

Employers are obliged to check every single employee's Right to Work in the UK, regardless of where they were born, and this includes those with British passports. There are strict guidelines for how to do this and employers have to see original documents and keep copies. Since January 2019, the Home Office has offered an online service that enables employers to view a job applicant's Right to Work. This involves the applicant completing an online application form and being issued with a code, which they give to the employer. The employer then logs on with the applicant's date of birth and code to verify the Right to Work. The employer must keep a copy of the check they have carried out.

There are different rules in place for Irish citizens, so it is important to ensure you have the correct information if you are employing anyone from Ireland.

More information and links to the website can be found at:

gov.uk/government/publications/preventing-illegal-working-guidance-for-employers-october-2013

gov.uk/view-right-to-work

gov.uk/government/publications/right-to-work-checks-employers-guide

Covid-19

As of 17th November 2021, the British government is reporting that there have been 166,730 deaths with Covid-19 on the death certificate and 9,675,058 people have tested positive in the UK since the virus was first identified and tested for.[25]

I could be writing about any pandemic here, but as we all know Covid-19 (Severe Acute Respiratory Syndrome Coronavirus 2 (SARS-CoV-2)) has been a global pandemic unlike anything seen since the Spanish flu of 1918. There was and is no rule book. Employers, governments and health advisors were all left making it up as they went along. The rules kept changing, new initiatives were quickly put in place and thousands of businesses pivoted. Some businesses have survived and risen bigger, stronger and better than before. Other businesses have struggled and continue to struggle, but with time and support will be ok. Unfortunately, there are also businesses that have failed. Many of these were already struggling and they just couldn't survive the lockdowns, restrictions and new waves that the pandemic threw at them.

Even as I write, we don't know what winter 2021/2 is going to throw at us. While 89% of those over 16 have had their first vaccinations and 81.6% have had both doses, there is still 1 in 10 people who remain unvaccinated in the UK and this will continue to pose problems for employers.

---

[25] coronavirus.data.gov.uk/

Addressing the elephant

I address hybrid working later but getting employees back to work has been a huge challenge for employers. All employers opening up their workplaces have had to do so in compliance with Covid-19 guidance and restrictions. While some employees were more than happy to return to the workplace, others were not.

The most important element to consider is your duty of care towards all employees, including those who are vulnerable, become vulnerable or live with vulnerable people. Communication, accommodation, discussion, understanding and negotiation are all going to be vital in ensuring that everyone feels safe. One of the best ways to do this is to ask employees for their input. Get them to answer questions about what they want and what would make them feel safe. Ask for ideas on making their workplace feel safer. Share your risk assessments with the team and demonstrate the measures you have put in place to keep everyone safe. Keep these risk assessments up to date and reissue them as they are updated. There is one theory that says we have to learn to live with Covid-19 and, as an employer, you need to learn to work with it, too.

If you have staff who are refusing to return to the workplace, you need to understand why and look at whether adjustments can be made. They may have the right to request flexible working, but more about this later.

Masks are contentious. It is still debateable whether they provide any real protection and if they do, which types and how much protection do they afford the wearer and those around them.

Unless the government determines otherwise, which it may do from time to time, it is going to be up to you as the employer to decide what your company rules are around the wearing of masks. This will need to be written into your risk assessments, company contracts, handbooks and dress code. It may be that you require masks in some areas of the building, but not others. It may be that you require people moving around to wear them, but not once someone is sat at their desks. It may be that if your staff are going into clients' homes or onto clients' premises, you have a policy that covers those circumstances.

Again, ask your staff for their input. It doesn't mean you have to implement their suggestions, but at least you know what their reaction is likely to be when you make your decisions. Whatever you determine your policy to be, document it, communicate it and enforce it. If you allow people to choose, ensure everyone feels comfortable with their personal decisions and they are not made to feel awkward. If you require people to wear masks, ensure there are consequences for those who don't. Remember, some people can't wear masks, so always investigate 'rebels' before labelling them as such and taking any action.

Vaccinations, although widely recognised by many as our way out of lockdown and restrictions, are not acceptable to everyone. As a country that does not generally mandate vaccinations, it is not possible for employers to require all employees to be vaccinated.

We have talked above about protected beliefs above and although not yet tested in the ET, I do think that people who can demonstrate that their stance against vaccinations is a long-held belief will be protected. At the present time, the government is just beginning to mandate vaccinations for care staff and potentially for NHS staff. In these settings, employers will be able to insist that staff are vaccinated, but if anyone else tries to hire or fire based on vaccination status, they might find themselves in the ET.

As with many things HR, talk to the staff who are unvaccinated, understand their position and recommend they speak to their GP or another medical professional. Like with other medical discussions, you are unlikely to be qualified to provide medical advice and it is not your job to do so. You can, however, signpost concerned employees in the right direction.

Again, you need to ensure that unvaccinated staff are not bullied or harassed as a result of their stance. They can't be excluded from the office or subject to any detriment because of their beliefs.

Schools and childcare have become huge issues for many working parents and especially women. Now that the worst of the lockdowns is over and the schools are back in person, it is important that you continue to support working parents with their ongoing childcare needs. It is not acceptable that a parent is working from home while looking after a young child. If your staff are working, then they need to be 100% present at work, regardless of where they are physically based. While care needs to be taken not to ostracise working parents, you do have the right to insist that they work when they are supposed to be working in the way you expect them to be working.

If an employee is unable to fulfil their contractual obligations, then either their contract needs to change (which it could do under flexible working) or other arrangements need to be put in place. Don't be scared to have difficult conversations. If you can hear a baby crying or see young children running around, have a direct discussion and address the elephant in the room. Ask what support they need and help them to work through the issues.

If they are contracted to be in the office, you can require them to come in at any point and failure to do so would put them in breach of contract. You obviously don't want to upset all your working parents, but you have a business to run, so work together to find a suitable solution.

At the moment, effects of long Covid-19 are still a bit unknown. It appears to affect people of all ages, including children, and the symptoms vary between individuals, but may include extreme tiredness, shortness of breath, chest pains or palpitations, join pain, sickness and loss of appetite, loss of taste or smell, rashes, depression and anxiety.

Some of the symptoms may become debilitating and if an employee is struggling with Long Covid-19 for months, they could then be protected by disability legislation. Look at ways in which you can accommodate the employee. If they are not well enough to work, then they should be on sick leave. If they are well enough to work but need to work from home or work shorter days, then these would be reasonable adjustments that should be accommodated, if possible.

Talk to the employee. Understand what they are going through, what medical support they are getting and if necessary, liaise with their GP or an occupational health practitioner. Just like any other employee with a long-term health issue, you need to address the elephant in the room and work together to find a solution that works for everyone.

Additional information

There is a lot of information about Covid-19 on both the government and the NHS websites. The rules are constantly changing, not only in an employment context, but also within society. It is important that you get proper advice and remain compliant as the situation evolves.

There is a lot of talk about society and the world of work being changed forever as a result of Covid-19. Some of this is being led by the uncertainty and some of it by the media, politicians, employers, trade unions and the employees themselves.

Although Covid-19 has moved organisations further and faster than they ever thought possible, I am not convinced that all the changes are here to stay. Legislation, Brexit and the climate crisis will all be thrown into the mix and although Covid-19 is a factor for change, it is not the only one.

Flexible working

Working parents with at least 26 weeks of service were first given the right to request flexible working in April 2003.[26]

At the time of writing, there is a proposal for all employees to have the right to request flexible working from day one of employment. I am outspoken on this subject and although a very strong advocate of flexible working, and have indeed had most of my employees over the years working flexibly both in terms of their hours and their work location, I am absolutely against this being legislated for.

I actively encourage our clients to think about whether a role can be full time or part time, whether it can be a job share and whether it can be home-based or at least hybrid, but there are some instances where this is not possible, practical or desirable by the business. I don't think that employers should be forced by legislation to do something that isn't right for their business or threatened with an ET when an employee doesn't get their own way. Don't be naïve enough to think this doesn't happen. We see at least two cases a month!

Addressing the elephant

The way in which you address this will in a large part be dependent on what happens with legislation. How much you are forced to do and how much you choose to do will come down to getting the right mix between legislation, culture and values. It will also depend on the nature of your business, your sector norms and your company goals. The legislation tends to

---

[26] The Employment Rights Act 2002

set minimum standards and businesses can choose to go above and beyond when writing their own policies and procedures.

The most important thing is to involve your staff in decisions about what is possible, feasible, practical and affordable. Create a culture in which everyone feels valued and in which there is an element of give and take. An example of this may be to allow someone to work from home if they have a sick child, to work through their lunch break to leave early for a medical appointment or to have a day off if they have had to work over the weekend. Some companies already manage this type of flexibility very well without the need for contractual changes.

A more permanent change to an employee's terms and conditions/contract of employment may be a permanent change in hours, a change to working days or working from home two days per week. I recommend that you set parameters to enable your business to function effectively, i.e. the office must be staffed between 8:30 and 5:30 Monday to Friday, no one can be alone in the office, everyone must work at least 20 hours per week, everyone must be in the office on a Monday for training, team meetings and supervisions, etc. Then if employees are requesting changes, they know what is possible and acceptable, as you have managed expectations.

Flexible working will help you to attract and retain people with the skills you need, those who share your values and will help to make the business more successful. However, the tail cannot wag the elephant; you should not be held to ransom as a result of flexible working and currently this is my fear.

Suppose you advertise a job as three days, Monday to Wednesday, because you have someone working Wednesday to Friday, and you hire someone to cover those 21 hours, 9am–5pm, Monday to Wednesday. When they arrive at 9am on Monday morning, they then inform you that under flexible working, they now want to work four hours per day, Monday–Friday from 8:30 to 12:30. This doesn't work for your business; you are not open at 8:30, you don't need cover on Thursday and Friday, etc; but the big question now is, what happens next? Can you fail the person's probation as they are refusing to work the hours they were hired to work? Do you have to change the working hours of other employees? If you do fail their probation, what protection rights will they have? Currently, an employee needs two years of service before they can bring certain claims in the ET; but will this remain the case? If the person needs the working hours for childcare reasons or mental health reasons, will this give them grounds for an indirect sexual discrimination claim or a disability claim – neither of which require any length of service and for which the compensation is unlimited?

Flexible working may well be the biggest elephant in the room in the coming years, but the devil will be in the detail and if there is ever a second edition of this book, then I'm certain that this chapter will change significantly.

Additional information

By the time this book is published, the consultation period for the amendments to the Flexible Working Act 2014 will have closed. It is possible that legislation will be in final draft, but whether it is introduced in 2022 or 2023 I cannot say.

Under the 2014 Act, the key points of the legislation are as follows:

- Employees need 26 weeks' service before they can submit a request for flexible working
- They can only submit one flexible working request per 12-month period, unless company policy increases the number of requests allowed per 12-month period

- Employers must respond within three months
- The change, if agreed, is a permanent change to the contract of employment
- There are eight reasons an employer can turn down a flexible working request:
  1. Extra cost that will burden the business
  2. The work cannot be reorganised among other staff – skills or time
  3. People cannot be recruited to do the work – the hours left to be covered are unpractical
  4. Flexible working will negatively affect quality
  5. Flexible working will negatively affect performance
  6. The business's ability to meet customer demand will be negatively affected
  7. There is a lack of work to do during the proposed working times
  8. The business is planning a structural change

The proposal being consulted on includes:
- Making the right to request flexible working a right from the first day of employment
- Revising or removing some or all of the eight reasons for rejecting a flexible working request
- Requiring the employer to suggest an alternative to the proposed flexible working request
- Allowing multiple requests within a 12-month period
- Making employers raise awareness of flexible working on a temporary or permanent basis
- Making flexible working the default working pattern
- Requiring employers to publish their flexible working policies

- Requiring employers to state whether flexibility will be considered when advertising jobs

Hybrid working

'We are not a team because we work together. We are a team because we respect, trust and care for each other.' [27]

This final chapter is focused specifically on businesses, or parts of businesses, that are usually office based, but have shifted far more to remote working as a result of lockdowns.

Anyone who tells you that they know what the future of work looks like is lying! If you had asked people two years ago if they would be working from home full-time within 12 months, the answer would have been a resounding 'no'. I've spent the last 25 years of my career helping employers to think about the options for allowing people to work remotely, and in 99% of cases, the answer was, 'We can't make it work.'

Now, just to put my cards on the table here, I started DOHR in 2007 and worked from home. I hired my first employees in April 2011 and, until 2014, we worked mostly from home, meeting up just once every two weeks around my dining room table. Laptops, a hosted server and VOIP phones meant we were seamless.

My husband, who is employed by a large multinational, has worked from home for the past 21 years. There is an office in the UK, but he is rarely there; if he was in any of his company's offices (pre-Covid-19), it was more likely to be one in the US. I guess he was the one who showed me that working from home could work.

Why did I get a small office in 2014? It certainly wasn't for use every day, but rather for storing products (by this stage I had developed our HR In A Box package), for printing professionally and for providing a space where the whole team

---

[27] *Vala Alshar, Chief Design Evangelist for Salesforce*

could work and collaborate, even if I was away. Up until mid-2020, I still had employees on home-worker contracts. Today, we have office-based contracts, but with the ability to work from home.

I don't have a crystal ball, but I am going to share some of the issues that I, my family and my clients have dealt with over the past year and that I can foresee persisting as problems in the post-Covid-19 business world.

The first is recruitment. We are humans, attuned to picking up on the nuances of body language. Only being able to see up someone's nose on a Zoom link that keeps cutting in and out is not the best way to interview them (although a background of their messy bed topped with yesterday's underwear can say a surprising amount about them).

Even if you start the process online, there is a tremendous amount of value to bringing them into the office, enabling them to do the journey, see the environment, feel the culture of the business and meet the team. Recruiting new team members without a single face-to-face meeting can lead to a significant rate of false starts. To minimise the expensive and disruptive risk of their employment failing, multiple interviews and a probation period are essential.

The second is training and development. My son is 20 and doing an internship this summer. He's been offered the choice of working from home, in the office or a mixture of the two. He's been told they no longer have enough desks in the department for everyone, so he may need to hot-desk. He doesn't care. He's going in. He wants to learn, listen, absorb, work with colleagues, and experience a 'normal' working life.

Training and development are essential elements in career and personal growth. I've had work-experience students who don't even know how to answer the phone. Observing how others work with clients and how people interact with each other, sitting in on meetings, asking a colleague to check an email all help build strong and trusted relationships, which are critical factors for success in business. Without the opportunity to work together, the opportunity for invaluable, informal learning is lost.

The workplace isn't just somewhere you go to work. For my brother and sister-in-law, and many like them, it's where they met. Without returning to the office, many working singles will also be missing out on a crucial element of their social life.

Many people have found that working from home fosters a healthier work-life balance, perhaps by cutting down the commute, by enabling a recharging lunch-hour walk or power nap, or simply by being at home when the kids get back from school. For others, the solitude of remote working has been unbearable. Perhaps due to the lack of human contact or proper workspace, such people are desperate to get back to the office and to their regular routines.

Where is the elephant?

Hybrid working can present employers and staff with a whole herd of these elephants. Here are some examples I've come across when advising clients throughout the pandemic.

Age

- Younger staff who are not vaccinated but want to be in the office
- Younger employees who are living in flat shares or bedsits and lack the space to work comfortably from home
- Older staff who may have health issues and don't want to work alongside others

Mental health
- The anxiety of travelling to work on public transport
- The seclusion of working from home and not having any contact with others
- The loss of routine and structure
- The merging of work and home life

Domestic abuse
- For some, work is their safe space and being at home exposes them to increased risk from their abuser

Sexual harassment
- If someone is working from home, they are less likely to be sexually harassed by a colleague
- However, if they are subjected to sexual harassment during an unrecorded phone call or video conference, it will be much harder for other colleagues or management to see what is going on and take the necessary actions

Bullying
- There may be less scope for bullying to occur when the team aren't physically together
- However, a bully can still operate on social media, Teams, Slack or on other communication channels with less risk of being detected
- It's much harder for a victim of bullying to come forward if they have no witnesses, and therefore their line manager is less likely to be aware of the situation, until it explodes

Smell

- In a LinkedIn poll I did earlier this year, the biggest HR elephant in the room was body odour. People with a BO problem may be more comfortable working from home, as they are usually self-conscious.
- By extension, it's also probably more pleasant for team members not to be around a colleague smelling of BO.

Drugs and alcohol

- If an employee has a drug or alcohol problem but is working from home, it's much harder for the business to identify and manage the situation.
- If someone is behaving oddly, you may put it down to lack of training or incompetence because you're missing vital cues that are easier to spot face-to-face – including, of course, the tell-tale smell.

THE FINAL WORD

With every HR elephant, company culture and communication are key.

Whether people are working from home or in the office, business owners are responsible for managing their staff effectively not only to ensure the business thrives, but also to ensure their employees are appropriately supported, nurtured and valued. This creates a virtuous circle with employees wanting to make a positive contribution to company success, rather than just coming along for the ride.

THE ELEPHANT RESOURCES

Your Elephant Scorecard

Before you start on your journey, you need to know where you are and have a plan. This scorecard will give you your personalised results and help you to draw up your route map.

https://dohr-elephant.scoreapp.com/

Your Elephant Field Guide

Here you will find useful downloads, templates and resources to help you identify and address the elephant in your workplace room.

www.dohr.co.uk/elephant-resources

The Head Ranger

You can send me your questions, thoughts or feedback at any time via twitter @dohr or by email at donna@dohr.co.uk

To enquire about a free 20-minute HR consultation, email Frank@dohr.co.uk

ABOUT THE AUTHOR

Donna Obstfeld graduated from the University of Hertfordshire with a joint honours degree in Business and Psychology. She is a Chartered Fellow of the Chartered Institute of Personnel and Development (FCIPD) and an accredited mediator.

Donna now writes on Human Resources issues for a number of publications and provides expert commentary on HR and business issues on the radio.

Donna was voted among the top 10 business mums in the 'Expert in their field' category of the mums club's The Business Mum Awards 2012. In February 2015 Donna's HR practice was named HR Consultancy of the year by the HR community at the HR Distinction awards and in 2017, Donna was recognised by Sage as one of the UK's top 100 Global Business Influencers.

Donna does not use the term HR Consultant or HR Manager when describing herself; she is a businesswoman first and foremost and her specialisation happens to be human resources – the management of people within a business and for the success of that business. As many of Donna's clients have discovered, this expertise and approach brings their business significant added value.

To find out more about Donna and her HR Practice, DOHR, visit dohr.co.uk

To book a free 20-minute HR consultation, email Frank@dohr.co.uk

TESTIMONIALS

"In today's busy business environment, it is all too easy to forget that people buy from people. Good networkers and good business owners know this. Therefore, you need to ensure that you are looking after them and looking after your business - they go together. As an expert in HR, Donna knows this too. This book is an indispensable guide for business owners looking to get to grips with their biggest asset."

Charlie Lawson,
National Director, UK & Ireland, BNI

"Donna is an expert in her field and a force to be reckoned with. She gets to know each business as if it were her own allowing her to make individualised recommendations based on each organisation's internal goals and culture. Donna's knowledge of employee relations and HR are exceptional and she has the extra dimension of being personable, practical and commercially savvy enabling her to provide expedient, high quality, solution-driven advice."

Fiona Mendel,
Employment Solicitor

'I've read this book and love the elephant theme. I admire how you've framed things, they ARE the elephants in the world of work. They are controversial, toxic, damaging, and even in many cases avoided. The world needs a compendium of these in one place.'

Perry Timms
Founder, People and Transformational HR